WE ARE THE NEW RADICALS

Lose the clutter, find your Life!

Purpose, Passion + Profit.

p16 "How much do we really need?

What really matters

Sentiment not moment action is the ruin of a soul.

Find your Beach!

⇒ when I am old - I think of all such things - simplify

Nature unimpeded is magic

A Manifesto for Reinventing Yourself and Saving the World

WE ARE THE NEW RADICALS

Julia Moulden

May 2008
for Aynsley
with heartfelt thanks!
Julia

McGraw Hill

New York Chicago San Francisco
Lisbon London Madrid Mexico City
Milan New Delhi San Juan Seoul
Singapore Sydney Toronto

The McGraw-Hill Companies

1 2 3 4 5 6 7 8 9 0 DOC/DOC 0 9 8 7

ISBN 978-0-07-149630-8
MHID 0-07-149630-0

McGraw-Hill books are available at special quantity discounts to use as premiums and sales promotions, or for use in corporate training programs. For more information, please write to the Director of Special Sales, Professional Publishing, McGraw-Hill, Two Penn Plaza, New York, NY 10121-2298. Or contact your local bookstore.

This book is printed on recycled, acid-free paper.

Library of Congress Cataloging-in-Publication Data
Moulden, Julia.
We are the new radicals / by Julia Moulden.
p. cm.
Includes bibliographical references and index.
ISBN-13: 978-0-07-149630-8 (alk. paper)
ISBN-10: 0-07-149630-0 (alk. paper)
1. Social action. 2. Social participation. 3. Social entrepreneurship.
I. Title.
HN18.3.M68 2008
303.48'4—dc22

2007043922

For my mother,
Dollie Helen Pauline Ritchie Moulden

And my niece,
Emma Margaret Moulden Tipler

CONTENTS

ACKNOWLEDGMENTS

As I began to write, Canadian theater legend John Van Burek sent me this Thomas Berger quote: "Why do writers write? Because it isn't there."

The analogy to Everest was fitting. I wrote this book because I knew from personal experience that nothing existed to help people like me transform our lives. And like any adventurer, I knew that my trip—despite its solitary nature—would not be made alone. I have many people to thank.

Thanks to the New Radical pioneers, first and foremost, for their candor and willingness to share their stories (more about them below). And also to my clients, who chose me as their trusted partner.

Thanks, too, to the impossibly wonderfully named Mollie Glick, smart cookie and dream agent; the exceptional team at McGraw-Hill, led by editorial director Jeanne Glasser, who got the concept immediately and helped me bring it to life; and Herb Schaffner, McGraw-Hill's business books publisher, a classic New Radical Innovator.

To my front line—Ilda Cardoso, Mark Dreu, Jennifer East, Mahalia Freed, Sherry Lowe-Bernie, Kye Marshall, Nedar Mendoza, Ara Melkonian, Paula Nieuwstraten, Umberto Pupo, Warren Sheffer, and Will Smith—my heartfelt appreciation.

I'm also grateful to early believers and strong supporters: My family, Mum, Rick, Elizabeth, Jeff, Ruth, Philip, Sean, and Emma. And friends, near and far, including Arax Acemyan, Rick Archbold, John Beck, Diana Bragman, Rick Byun, Nancy Chafee, Russ Christianson, Raynald Desmeules, Katherine East, Jonathan Ezer, Elizabeth Fairley, Eric Flint, Rosanne Freed, Reuben Freed, Jeremy Freed, Nancy Gipson, Alison Hardacre, Lynne Heller, Latimer Kells, Julia Kelly, Paul Kent, Malcolm Lester, Brent Lowe-Bernie, Jaimie Macpherson, Hillary McMahon, Chris Oliver, Kerry Peacock, Tralee Pearce, Bruce Piercey, Carl Safina, Madeline Thompson, Catherine Thompson, Anne Van Burek, Louise Walker, Tom Williams, and Rick Wester.

My thanks to the New Radicals Salon circle; my ever-patient Bee's Knees clients; my thoughtful neighbors; and Day, Sim, and Gav, because you are never far from my mind.

My deepest thanks to the following New Radicals:

Peter C. Alderman Foundation
www.petercaldermanfoundation.org

POA Educational Foundation
www.poafoundation.org

Adrian Bradbury and
Kieran Hayward, GuluWalk
www.guluwalk.com

Mark Brayne
www.braynework.com

Bring Light
www.bringlight.com

Bridgestar
www.bridgestar.org

Canada Pension Plan
Investment Board
www.cppib.ca

Carnegie Institution
www.globalecology.standford.edu

Dart Center
www.dartcenter.org

Ron Dembo, Zerofootprint
www.zerofootprint.net

Ensemble Capital
www.ensemblecapital.com

Tactical Philanthropy
www.tacticalphilanthropy.com

Exquisite Safaris
www.exquisitesafaris.com

Games for Change
www.gamesforchange.org

The Global Fund to Fight AIDS, Tuberculosis and Malaria
www.theglobalfund.org

Grameen Foundation
www.grameenfoundation.org

Guelph Civic League
www.guelphcivicleague.ca

Heart and Stroke Foundation
www.heartandstroke.ca

Imagine Canada
www.imaginecanada.ca

Institute for OneWorld Health
www.oneworldhealth.org

KaosPilots International
www.kaospilot.dk

Jamie Kennedy
www.jamiekennedy.ca

Kids Internet Safety Alliance
www.kinsa.net

Sierra Club
www.sierraclub.org

Stephen Lewis Foundation
www.stephenlewisfoundation.org

Stephon Marbury
www.nba.com

Kye Marshall
www.kyemarshall.com

Motto Magazine
www.whatsyourmotto.com

Myelin Repair Foundation
www.myelinrepair.org

NAACP
www.naacp.org

North South Project
www.northsouthproject.com

Notre Dame de Namur University
www.ndnu.edu

Dan O'Brien
www.wildideabuffalo.com

Right to Play
www.righttoplay.com

Roots of Empathy
www.rootsofempathy.org

Stanley-Bostitch
www.stanleyworks.com

Surf City Growers
www.surfcitygrowers.com

Teach for America
www.teachforamerica.org

Ubuntu Edmonton
www.ubuntuedmonton.org

World University Service of Canada
www.wusc.ca

World Bank
www.worldbank.org

Finally, my thanks to the "guests" included in the Coda (Bonus Chapter 1), in the order in which they are introduced.

Norman Borlaug
www.normanborlaug.org

Cary Fowler, Global Crop Diversity Trust
www.croptrust.org

Gehendra Gurung, Practical Action
www.itdg.org

Anna Lappé and Bryant Terry, *Grub*
www.smallplanetinstitute.org

Retired Navy Vice Admiral Conrad C. Lautenbacher, Jr., GEONETCast
www.earthobservations.org

Dennis McGuire, Ecosphere Technologies
www.ecospheretech.com

Anshul Garg, Mokshda Paryavaran Evam Van Suraksha Samiti
www.mokshda.org

Patrick Hettiaratchi, University of Calgary
www.schulich.ucalgary.ca

Wayne Dunn, Clark Sustainable Resource Developments
www.csrdevelopments.com

Mathew Cherian, HelpAge International
www.helpage.org

Andrea and Barry Coleman, Riders for Health
www.riders.org

Dr. Sonika Verma, Council of Scientific and Industrial Research
www.csir.res.in

Jessica Kerwin, Anandwan
www.anandwan.org

Cees Buisman, Wetsus
www.wetsus.nl

Dr. Gerhard Knies, Coordinator of TREC
www.TRECers.net

Dr. Franz Trieb, Project Manager for the TRANS-CSP
www.dlr.de/tt/trans-csp

Dave Shepard, Sky WindPower
www.skywindpower.com

Jürgen Schmid, Institute of Solar Energy Technology
www.solarenergy.ch

Dennis McGrew, NatureWorks
www.natureworksllc.com

Brinda Dlala, Xerox
www.xerox.com

Ian Yolles, Nau
www.nau.com

Nicholas Negroponte, One Laptop Per Child
www.laptop.org
www.XOgiving.org

Robert Tolmach, Changing the Present
www.changingthepresent.org

Loki Osborn, Elephant Pepper Development Trust
www.elephantpepper.org

Farouk Jiwa, Honey Care Africa
www.honeycareafrica.com

Mark Finser, RSF Social Finance Bank
www.rsfsocialfinance.org

Robert Chambers, Bonnie CLAC
www.bonnieclac.org

Matt and Jessica Flannery, Kiva.org
www.kiva.org

Christopher Crane, Opportunity International Micro Insurance Agency
www.opportunity.org

Ken Livingstone,
Mayor of London, England
www.london.gov.uk

Bernard Lietaer, Access Foundation
www.accessfoundation.org

Eric Bigot, Architect
www.zenkaya.com

Tye Farrow, Architect
www.farrowpartnership.com

Travis Price, Architect and Educator
www.travispricearchitects.com

Ann Dowling, Cambridge University
www.eng.cam.ac.uk

Zoltan Spakovsky, Massachusetts Institute of Technology
www.mit.edu/engineering

Margaret Atwood, Author
www.longpen.com

Tom Ritchey, Cargo bike designer
www.projectrwanda.org

Daryn Kagan
www.darynkagan.com

Bishop Kevin Dowling, South Africa
www.catholic-hierarchy.org/diocese

Richard Chartres, Bishop of London, Church of England
www.london.anglican.org

Thich Nhat Hanh, Zen Master
www.plumvillage.org

Gil Frondsal, Zen Priest
www.sati.org

Rabbi Michael Lerner, Network of Spiritual Progressives
www.spiritualprogressives.org

Carlos Leite, Librarian, Jardim Catarina, Brazil

Saad Eskander,
Baghdad National Library, Iraq
www.bl.uk/iraqdiar

Rory Stewart,
Turquoise Mountain Foundation
www.turquoisemountain.org

Hellen Ayek, Ugandan women's shelter

Somaly Mam, AFESIP
www.afesip.org

Adha Goswami, Ladli, India
www.ladli.org

John Hickenlooper, Mayor of Denver, Colorado
www.denvergov.org

Craig Kielburger, Free the Children
www.freethechildren.com

Walter Cronkite and Ohio Congressman Dennis Kucinich, U.S. Department of Peace
www.thepeacealliance.org
www.kucinich.house.gov

Council of Elders
www.worldcouncilofelders.org

Chapter 1

Are You a New Radical?

The latest source of global warming worry? Funeral pyres in India. Each year, 8.5 million Hindus are cremated. An adult body requires as much as 500 kg [kilograms, about 1,100 pounds] of wood and as long as six hours to burn. Estimates peg the annual contribution to global warming of this ancient tradition at 7 million tonnes [7,716,179 tons] of carbon dioxide.

—*The Economist*, June 2007

"That our world is in trouble is not news.

This morning, I flipped through the two dailies that appear on my doorstep before dawn.

- More bloodshed in Iraq and Afghanistan.
- A week of brutal warfare has isolated the Palestinian territories.
- New horrors in Zimbabwe, Somalia, and the Sudan.
- Children taken from their homes to work as sex slaves and laborers.
- A corporate corruption trial is underway in Chicago.
- A team of researchers that is traversing the Arctic is getting a sobering look at how global warming is changing the landscape.

But wait. There is also the story about a man in Florida who has developed a portable water-filtration system that is powered by a small wind turbine and foldout solar panels. Such a machine would be a real boon for refugee camps, remote medical clinics, and anywhere that safe drinking water is in short supply. "It's water in a box," Ecosphere Technologies founder Dennis McGuire says simply.

He doesn't know it yet, but Dennis is part of an emerging movement of people who are reinventing their work to help save the world. It's a movement based on a powerful new idea: that doing good can mean more than volunteering and philanthropy. How we *earn our living* can actually become the way we give back. I call these men and women *New Radicals.*

Where did this idea come from, and how did this movement get started? It all began with the largest and most successful generation the world has ever known: the baby boomers. There are

80 million boomers in North America alone, and that generation has been busy lately: pursuing careers, raising families, putting down roots. Now, at midlife, boomers like me are lifting our heads, looking around, and wondering what comes next. We know we'll live longer than any previous generation, and we're simply not interested in retirement. In fact, we're feeling at the top of our game. But now we want something more from our work. We want it to reflect our values and to help us make a difference in the world. Probe a little, and we'll share what's closest to our hearts: we believe that our greatest contribution is yet to come. And we may be right—we now have the expertise, knowledge, and resources to do what we once only dreamed of.

All around us, the rich and powerful are doing good works. The names are familiar to everyone, and each new gesture is more astonishing than the last. But does that mean that you have to be worth billions in order to become a New Radical? No. Can ordinary people like you and I transform how we earn our daily bread? Absolutely.

I say this with confidence because I did. After 20 years as a self-employed speechwriter—work I enjoyed immensely, and for which I was well paid—I was feeling restless. I didn't want to do the same thing for the next two decades, but I had no idea what might come next. I scarcely acknowledged it at first, but I found myself thinking about my youth, when school friends and I would talk late at night about how we would change the world. What happened to that young woman? And could I somehow combine her ideals and dreams with the mature, experienced professional I'd become? Gradually, I realized that I was not alone, that many of my peers were having similar thoughts and also longing for more meaning. And if I couldn't find resources to help me transform myself, well, neither could they. Suddenly it became clear. My journey could be combined with my expertise (a lifetime of listening to others and helping them turn their vision into words) to create the core of a new practice. Today, I'm a midlife coach helping boomers make the transition to the second half of their working lives.

Over the last several years, I have talked and worked with scores of men and women who are reinventing what they do and have discovered that there is a fantastic variety of ways to become a New Radical—think of it as a continuum between "mildly" and "wildly" radical. New Radicals are appearing in every sector and in countries around the world. While the possibilities are endless, the roles that New Radicals are choosing fall into three categories: Activists, Entrepreneurs, and Innovators.

Activists are those who actively serve the less fortunate. For example, they may move from the corporate to nonprofit sector, or carve significant time out of their busy schedules to take on a second, helping role. They are people like Kye Marshall, who left a comfortable seat playing cello for a major orchestra to become a music psychotherapist. Kye now works with women with special needs, such as those with eating disorders. Another Activist is Aditya Jha, who developed a program pairing aboriginal youth with corporate executives to foster entrepreneurship and the development of business skills in native communities.

In contrast, *Entrepreneurs* start new enterprises where making a difference is an integral part of their work. They are people like Suzanne Seggerman of Games for Change, an organization that is a key player in the social games industry—that is, digital games that help people learn about social issues while entertaining them at the same time. Another is Ayisi Makatiani. Educated at the best U.S. schools, he moved to Africa to help launch the continent's first Internet service provider. Today, he is on a mission to promote development on the continent, one small business at a time.

And then there are the *Innovators,* people who change their current role or influence their field or organization from within. Innovators are people like Don Raymond, senior vice president and head of public market investments for the Canada Pension Plan Investment Board (CPPIB), which manages a fund that will help sustain the pension contributions of 16 million Canadians. At Don's suggestion, CPPIB joined a global coalition of investors seeking to incorporate environmental, social, and governance issues into their financial decision making. Willard (Dub) Hay, a senior vice president at Starbucks, is another Innovator who drove a corporate program to pay coffee producers a premium beyond the going rate. He's also behind another initiative that helps farmers through a combination of technical support and microfinance loans.

The bottom line is that, whether Activist, Entrepreneur, or Innovator, we can choose—or create—a role that works for us. This book tells the stories of the first wave of New Radicals: you'll read about the work they are doing and how they have transformed themselves. And while this movement was launched by North American boomers, you'll discover that it embraces people of all ages and from every part of the world.

How did I choose which men and women to include? I looked first for imaginative, creative, and compassionate people. Sometimes, I chose them for their work (was it constructive?) and sometimes for their approaches (were they positive and hopeful?). And I made sure to include examples that range from profound, life-altering transformations (the wild end of the spectrum) to more modest roles that are within reach of everyone, with stories from a variety of sectors and from different corners of the globe.

How did I find them? The first came from my own network. Others found me as word of what I was doing began to spread. And I discovered many of them through the media. (Now that you're aware of the New Radicals movement, don't be surprised if you start discovering examples in your favorite news source on a regular basis.) You won't have heard of most of these people, and that's just how they like it. The majority of New Radicals I interviewed began our conversation with the deeply humble question: "But why have you chosen me?" They wanted me—and you—to know instead about the work they are doing, the wonderful people they have come to know, and how each of us can make a difference.

The question I hear most often from people like you is, "How can I become a New Radical?" It was immediately clear to me that New Radicals have different motivations, take different journeys, and reach different destinations. But, as I spoke with them, a pattern began to emerge. I realized that they had asked themselves a similar series of questions: "What's going on inside me?" "What is it I have to offer the world?" "What might my new role be?" and "How am I going to get there from here?" Each chapter tackles one of the questions New Radicals ask and shares the answers that helped them move forward. In this New Radical manifesto, I outline how to join the movement that is sweeping the world.

If you're wondering whether (or hoping that) becoming a New Radical is easy, I have to break it to you: it's not. While some made quick, relatively stress-free transitions, for most people the process was long and difficult. They worked hard, took considerable risks, and often faced substantial hurdles. But the rewards were equally profound. Seeing firsthand the fruits of their labor comes at the top of everyone's list. They also spoke about a sense of personal renewal—a feeling of exhilaration that comes with learning new things and exploring unfamiliar terrain.

One unanticipated but nearly universal benefit: new friendships. Tony Leighton, a freelance business writer and wildly successful community activist, said it best: "I now have a group of friends with whom I've shared a deep experience. They say that in war conditions are lousy, but when it's over, you miss it. When you do this work, you meet people who've been in those trenches, and they're the ones you want to spend time with."

The most common age, by the way? Fifty. I decided to include everyone's age in this book and so, as a gesture when asking for this information, would offer my own first. "I'm 50," I'd say. "How old are you?" "I'm 50, too!" was a frequent reply. And many then mentally calculated the ages of others in their organization or circle, and 50 came up time and again. Perhaps the saying "don't trust anyone over 30" has evolved into the boomer-friendly "your new life begins at 50."

Here are some other numbers to contemplate. Just how large might this movement be? Let's take North American baby boomers as our starting point—leaving aside, just for a moment, New Radicals who are older and younger than this generation, as well as New Radicals from other countries. As I said, there are about

80 million in North America. Studies such as the Merrill Lynch New Retirement Survey show that as much as 75 percent of this generation intends to keep working. And of this group, more than 60 percent say they want to do good works now. A conservative estimate of the number of New Radicals-in-the-making? Thirty million.

Somehow, without conferring with one another, but guided by the same experiences and influences, New Radicals have collectively chosen a new occupation: saving the world. What will happen as this movement develops self-awareness and picks up speed? We are already seeing the difference individual New Radicals can make. It only makes sense that our collective and cumulative impact will be unprecedented. In the next few decades, we have a remarkable opportunity—as individual human beings and as an international family—to realize our full potential and, in doing so, to solve many of the problems that face us.

Chart Your Course
While reading this book—or when you're ready to begin your own New Radical journey—you might find the check-ins and reflections beginning on page 223 helpful.

This chapter poses the first question: "Are you a New Radical?" By now you know enough about the New Radical profile and the kinds of things they are doing to answer the question. If you shouted "yes!" or even if you're just a little bit curious, I invite you to read on. You're embarking on a voyage that will certainly influence the way you see the world, and it may just change your life.

Chapter 2

How Do You Get Started?

By 2008, more than half the world's population—3.3 billion people—will live in towns and cities, and the number is expected to swell to almost five billion by 2030, according to a United Nations Population Fund report. Poverty is increasing more rapidly in urban areas . . . a billion people . . . already live in slums.

—*New York Times*, June 2007

What made you pick up this book? If you're like most people, it's because you want your work to be more meaningful. And it can be, as the New Radicals you'll meet will testify. But thinking about it is one thing, actually taking the plunge is something else entirely.

What is it that makes people leave a job that they are good at and try to do something new? What force is so powerful that it propels us outside our comfort zone and onto an uncertain path? It may surprise you to learn that the motivation is personal. Many emerging New Radicals are deeply embarrassed to admit that they didn't wake up one morning with a burning desire to save the world. Relax, I tell them gently. I can't say that no one gets started that way, but the people who do are few and far between.

Instead, New Radicals—Activists, Entrepreneurs, and Innovators alike—experience a kind of wake-up call: an internal voice or an external event that announces the end of one part of your life, and the beginning of another. I've observed three categories of wake-up call. Just like the wind, the force they exert on our lives varies depending on their velocity. There is Level One, a gentle whisper; Level Two, which is much louder and more insistent; and Level Three, which is the most unequivocal of all.

Tools for Your Journey
Check-ins and reflections to help guide your journey begin on page 225.

LEVEL ONE: STIRRED

The first wake-up call is a gentle nudge, an invitation to rouse ourselves. An inner voice says something like, "Okay, this work is no longer enough. It's time for something more." You've heard this call—or something like it—or you wouldn't be reading this book. When men and women end up on my couch after this most benign of signals, I begin by praising them because the vast majority ignore the first alarm. It takes a giant wallop before most people—including me—respond.

What kinds of things do people say when they plop down in front of me? "I'm about to turn 50 (or 40, or 60). What am I going to do with the rest of my life?" Sometimes they talk about a growing sense of mortality and that they are thinking about how they want to be remembered. Georgina Steinsky-Schwartz is a case in point. Throughout her career, Georgina moved easily between the private, public, and nonprofit sectors, always looking for a way to have an impact, but now it was time for something quite specific to this new phase of her life. "In my fifties, I realized the time had come for a legacy project." Today, she is president and CEO of Imagine Canada, a national program to promote public and corporate giving and volunteering. And Tony Leighton, the affable and articulate copywriter-cum-community activist we met in Chapter 1 was clear that he didn't want his legacy to be about the magazine awards he'd won or the thousands of "really stirring" corporate brochures he'd written. He wanted people to know he'd done good works, too. "'He led a rich and varied life, and he spent a good portion of it helping other people and the common good' would be a wonderful thing to carve on my headstone."

Other New Radicals-in-the-making told me that they suddenly felt that the work they once loved no longer appealed to them. My reply was an arched eyebrow and a compassionate, "Join the club!" After all, we've been building our careers for decades—many of us doing variations on a theme for a very long time. The work can't possibly be as interesting as it once was. Even those of us who got dream jobs hit the wall at some point. In the liner notes for a compact disc she compiled for Starbucks, the singer and songwriter Joni Mitchell wrote: "By the end of the 20th century, it seemed to me that the muse had gone out of music, and all that was left was the 'ic.' Nothing sounded genuine or original . . . I quit the business." She went on to say that she volunteered for the Starbucks project to remember what she had once loved about music. If Joni Mitchell could fall out of love with songs, where would that leave the rest of us?

Which was precisely how Melissa Dyrdahl was feeling when we sat down to talk. She began by describing how it dawned on her. For many years she'd loved working in the high-tech field. Her career followed the growth of Silicon Valley, culminating in a role as senior vice president of corporate marketing and communications for Adobe Systems. It was a stimulating environment, filled with interesting people, and with lots of opportunities for women. Then, one day, things changed. Her work lost its luster, a surprising and deeply distressing turn of events. "I found myself sitting in meetings, not being able to focus. At first, I tried putting it in the back of my mind, but it kept resurfacing. I can't tell you how upsetting it was. Everything I thought I wanted, the job that had made me so happy and energized and that once seemed so challenging and significant just wasn't anymore."

As Melissa discovered, a Level One can be distressing. But is it enough to set things in motion? Yes. At the age of 48, Kevin Salwen left a prestigious media job to pursue work that would use more of his abilities and add new depth to his life.

Kevin had been at the *Wall Street Journal* for 18 years, and he had risen to the top of the organization. One day, he began to notice subtle changes in his behavior: he was getting into work a little later, leaving a little earlier, and delegating more. He wasn't happy about it, telling his wife, Joan, that it could mean only one thing—that his work no longer challenged him and that he needed to do something about that. "I figured I was using 10 to 15 percent of my brain, at most. I knew it was time to make a change."

Staying at the *Journal* was one of the options Kevin considered. He went through a series of exercises in his head, but he realized there wasn't much left for him to do. So he quit his job and started a company with another *Journal* alumnus, Anita Sharpe. They launched their first venture at the height of the dot-com boom and did very well. Yet, all the while, they continued to talk about the changing media landscape. One day, they spotted a gaping hole in business journalism. "Traditional business magazines are all about strategy and operations—everything from the neck up." Kevin and Anita were both interested in creating more meaning and purpose in their lives, and personal experience coupled with research convinced them they weren't alone. They decided to launch a magazine that would speak to this growing audience. "It would be based on the idea that the heart and soul of a business is just as important as its brain."

And so *Motto* magazine was born. Its tagline is "Purpose, Passion, and Profit," and this guiding principle is something its cofounder takes very seriously. "Every day I walk into my office with a dual mission: to make the world a better place *and* to make money for our investors."

LEVEL TWO: SHAKEN

The second kind of wake-up call can take the form of an amped-up internal voice or a powerful external event. In some way, life comes unglued: we lose our jobs, discover we're seriously ill, or our marriage comes to an end.

When this happens, we are caught off guard by its suddenness and shaken by its intensity. Perhaps immediately, but more likely once the dust settles and we have a chance to catch our breath, we take a fresh look at our lives. One client described it to me this way: "It's like coming home after a long holiday, when everything that was once familiar looks somehow different."

New Radicals who experience a Level Two ask the same question—"How can I find work with more meaning?"—but they report a sense of urgency in coming up with an answer. Consider the case of Rocco Rossi.

Family legend has it that Rocco, age 45, has always been in a hurry. "My mother even says I was born with three teeth, 'In a hurry to eat!'" Rocco was in a hurry to finish school, to become president of a company, to buy the biggest house in the best part of town, and by his late thirties, he pretty much had it made. He was a senior executive with a global company, happily married, and living the good life. One day, he flew to Belgium for a series of meetings to prepare the company to go public. He traveled with his boss, the man who recruited him, and whom he idolized. "I thought, 'This is my goal in life, to be like this guy, so energetic, accomplished, [and with] an amazing family and all the toys.'" The meetings went well, and they celebrated one night, patting each other on the back, knowing they'd made a fortune. Rocco went down to breakfast the next morning, feeling on top of the world, and discovered that his boss had died in his sleep. "A massive coronary. At 44."

Even years later, Rocco's voice was thick with emotion. For the first time in his life, he questioned the pace he'd set so long ago. And, with his mentor gone, he discovered he simply wasn't interested in work. So, he took some time off and went as far away as he could. "I flew to New Zealand and spent a month circumventing the South Island—walking, cycling, and sea kayaking." One might assume that he would come home ready to change his life. But old habits die hard, and the successful businessman inside of him wasn't going anywhere. "On the way home, I had this little internal monologue going: 'What, are you going to throw yourself in the grave, too? Life goes on! There are still lots of opportunities . . .'" And, before long, he was back on the merry-go-round.

Rocco spent the next year taking a company from near bankruptcy to success, selling it, and making a tidy profit for himself and his investors. But he couldn't shake the feeling that, while it was a wonderful way to make a living, it was a terrible way to live. His reputation as "Chainsaw Rossi" meant success, but it also meant displaced people and broken dreams. While contemplating this second wake-up call, he came upon an article that would launch a deeper voyage of self-discovery. "Julia, it was really something. I was riding the subway one morning, reading the newspaper. I turned the page, and there's this article about the Camino Frances—you know, the trail that crosses northern Spain? I called the writer, took him out to lunch, and within a couple of weeks, I was on a plane to Pamplona."

Rocco likes to say he went for a walk. Some walk! Nine hundred kilometers (about 560 miles) along a route Christian pilgrims have followed for more than a thousand years. A month of solitude and physical challenge gave him time to think. And the necessity of carrying everything on his back gave him a metaphor for his reflections: how much do we really need? This time, the homecoming was different. Rocco knew that he was finished with the corporate world, unless he could find a company that shared his values. At the same time, the idea of public service was growing in him, and he started making the rounds, talking to people he knew, and checking in with several executive search firms. This is when he ran into something New Radicals have experienced a lot: although he'd had a stellar career, no one knew what to do with a guy who wanted to save the world. "I soon discovered that if you only have a vague sense of what you want to do—looking back, I realize I was pretty incoherent, talking about wanting to do good—no matter how bright or talented, or what your record is, they don't know what to do with you, and it represents too much of a risk to present you. I knew I needed clarity, but I had none."

He spent the next year working on a friend's mayoral campaign, which gave him hope that he, too, would find his way. "Here was a guy at the height of his business career, deciding to give it all up and devote himself to public service." Being his friend's campaign manager was fantastic—and a great learning opportunity, too. "It was extraordinary to watch my old friend, John Tory, learn the ropes, to see him grow into a completely different role." When John didn't win and instead decided to try his hand at provincial politics, Rocco chose not to follow (they're loyal to different parties). Instead, he did what was becoming a habit: he took a walk.

Rocco wanted to do some more thinking, and the theme of service got reinforced with each kilometer as he encountered locals along the way: "People came out of their homes along the Camino, offering water and food to passing pilgrims. These humble men and women always refused payment. Sometimes, though, they would ask me to pray for them when I reached Santiago, a place many of them would never see." Rocco was clear now that his New Radical role would be about service. Soon after, he was able to make another critical choice—that the nonprofit sector was where he wanted to work. Next, he enumerated the criteria such an organization would have to meet in order to be the right fit for him, including size, complexity, and a personal connection: "It would have to be large enough to offer a significant challenge and able to pay me a decent salary, because my son was still in school and I wanted him to be able to go to the university of his choosing. I also realized that there would have to be a meaningful link. As you know, a big chunk of what an executive in that sector does is raise funds. If I didn't have a personal commitment to the cause, it would be too easy to bail—to pull the rip cord—when things got tough."

His voice filled with emotion again as he told me that, one day, it just hit him—he got the clarity he had been struggling toward: "Of course! I'd lost my grandfather and mother-in-law to stroke, and my beloved boss—the man who had started me on this journey—to a heart attack." Today, Rocco is CEO of the Heart and Stroke Foundation of Ontario.

LEVEL THREE: DEVASTATION

For a small number of New Radicals, the starting point for their journey is absolutely brutal. I'm not talking about the standard losses and blows of life—these are the things that aren't supposed to happen. And when they do, they completely upend our lives and threaten to destroy us.

I first discovered Elizabeth and Stephen Alderman while reading the *New York Times* over the Christmas holidays. When I learned what had happened to them and how they responded, I burst into tears. And then I couldn't get to the phone fast enough. It takes something extraordinary to transform the greatest loss of all into a radically new way of being in the world, but that's precisely what Liz and Steve, both 65, have done.

Not long ago, they were living the American dream in Bedford, New York. Steve was a radiation oncologist, Liz a special education teacher, and they'd raised three wonderful children. And then, on September 11, 2001—9/11—their youngest son, Peter, died in the World Trade Center. And their carefully constructed world came crashing down. How does one cope with the unimaginable heartbreak of losing a child—and under such horrific circumstances? The Aldermans didn't want to dwell on their personal story when we spoke, but I can tell you this: within six months of Peter's murder (their choice of words), Steve retired from his profession, and Liz started seeing a psychiatrist to help her cope.

Very soon after, they knew that they wanted to do something to honor Peter's life. They considered and rejected a number of options, because nothing really captured their hearts. And then, sitting quietly one night, they turned on the television to watch the current affairs program *Nightline* and saw a story that would change the direction of their lives for the second time. It was about the victims of mass violence who are no longer able to function because of what happened to them.

Liz told me that there are a billion such people: "One sixth of the world's population is in this position. They've experienced torture, terror . . ."

"One billion?" I interrupted, trying to wrap my mind around the number.

"Yes, we have all the stats, and perhaps 60 to 70 percent of these people become emotionally paralyzed as a result of this trauma," Steve replied, and we all paused for a moment.

The Aldermans knew there was nothing they could do for Peter, but they felt they *could* do something for people who *survived* but were unable to get on with their lives. It was a perfect match. "We knew instantly that it was an ideal way to honor our son," Steve said. The next morning, they contacted Dr. Richard Mollica, director of the Harvard Program in Refugee Trauma (HPRT), whose work had been featured on the show, and within two weeks they were in his office. Mollica is a pioneer and international expert in the treatment of victims of mass violence. HPRT has collaborated with the United Nations and individual postconflict countries and established a global health policy to aid in the recovery and reconstruction of communities devastated by mass violence. He told the Aldermans what he dreamed of doing, but that he simply couldn't raise funds to move forward. "He's got a great track record at getting money from government and big foundations, but this new work was considered experimental, and that's much harder to fund," Liz said. "We told him we could help."

They created a foundation that would fund and administer their work with Dr. Mollica and allow them to take on new ventures as well. The Peter C. Alderman Foundation's mission is to "alleviate the suffering of victims of terrorism and mass violence in postconflict countries by providing indigenous caregivers with the tools to treat mental anguish using Western medical therapies combined with local healing traditions." Using a train-the-trainer model, they offer a master class series that shows caregivers how to treat victims. Once they have been certified as a master, these men and women go back to their countries and train 10 other people each month—teachers and midwives, shamans and village elders. And they always make sure to introduce local traditions into these teachings. Steve underlined this point: "Although posttraumatic stress and its treatment are universal, how trauma is presented varies according to culture. So, understanding that, and weaving these traditions in, is an essential part of what makes this work on the ground."

The foundation has trained 35 people from 12 countries on 4 continents, including Afghanistan, Bosnia and Herzegovina, Cambodia, Chile, Indonesia, Iraq, Macedonia, Rwanda, Spain, Srpska, and Uganda. Liz and Steve estimate that they've helped more than 50,000 people to date. And now, along with daughter Jane, the Aldermans are poised to do even more. They have opened the first Peter C. Alderman clinics in Uganda and Cambodia as a way to help more people, faster. And they plan to take their work on the road by taking local caregivers directly to refugee camps in places like northern Uganda. "Northern Uganda has seen civil war for 20 years," Steve told me. "These are people who desperately need help, and who simply can't travel 200 miles [322 kilometers] to a clinic."

Liz added with characteristic clarity: "These people have *nothing*. At least we know what happened to our son. My heart goes out to the parents of the 30,000 children who have been kidnapped in northern Uganda. They don't have a clue where their children are, or even if they are alive."

As we wrapped up our conversation, Steve added a final thought that neatly describes the heart of their mission: "We believe there was profound evil on 9/11. One of our board members put it best when he said that our work is to counter profound evil with profound good."

THE EXCEPTION TO THE RULE

For the very lucky few, the New Radical journey begins not with restlessness or outright misery, but with something quite the opposite. Some of the men and women I've met describe their awakening as like being hit by lightning. And that when it happens, everything is illuminated: they see quite clearly what they must do.

Scott Johnson, a veteran of the Boston Consulting Group and three Silicon Valley start-ups, talked to me about his bolt out of the blue. He had no grand plan for switching careers. Then, he was sitting in an airport lounge, on a day like any other, reading a business magazine, when his eyes fell on the smallest news item: "It was something really tiny, I mean, two paragraphs, that talked about MS [multiple sclerosis] and repair." But that brief article was enough to trigger an interest that changed his life. Scott quit his job and founded the not-for-profit Myelin Repair Foundation. It's a deeply personal mission: Scott was diagnosed with MS in 1976, and repairing myelin (the fatty coating that protects nerve cells, something those with MS lack) is the best hope for a cure.

In contrast, Nicole Pageau heard a speech that tore open her heart and laid the groundwork for a new life. Esther Mujawayo spoke in Edmonton, Canada, on the tenth anniversary of the Rwandan genocide. Listening to this powerful woman recount the horrors was difficult for Nicole, but what really touched her was learning about the survivors, especially the women. "She talked about the widows who'd been carrying on all these years, in total poverty, raising their children, and the orphans they'd adopted." Nicole was moved to tears and knew immediately that she wanted to help. Within 12 months, she'd started a one-woman nongovernmental organization (NGO), quit her job, sold everything she owned, and moved to Africa. She now helps the women of a small village on the outskirts of Kigali run several small businesses, including one that makes uniforms for a local college. When Nicole talked about changing her life and the work she is doing now, it sounded as though she was describing a love affair. I told her what I had observed, and she laughed softly.

"Yes, you could say it is the love of my life. My relationships with men didn't last. And now I know that I was destined for the love of a lot of women."

YOUR JOURNEY BEGINS

"Now," my clients sometimes say when I share New Radical stories like the ones in this chapter with them, "this kind of thing happens in every life. What makes New Radicals so different?" It's a question I asked myself: "Did I simply find people who stumbled into their new roles, or was there something distinctive about them that dramatically increased the likelihood that they would become New Radicals?" My answer is that there is a definite difference.

It's all in how these men and women responded to the shake-up. We can't control what life throws our way, but how we deal with the inevitable difficulties defines us. The people who would become New Radicals described what was going on in their lives—no matter how painful or disruptive—in positive terms: even as the world eroded under their feet, even as they faced an uncertain future, they believed that good would come of it. As I said earlier, once they had dusted themselves off and the air had begun to clear, they talked about being able to see themselves more vividly than they had in a long time—sometimes, as if for the very first time. They also spoke of the wake-up call as an opportunity to change their lives: "This isn't an escape from my old life, but a doorway to something new and more fulfilling." They described seeing the world as suddenly being full of possibilities. They knew that new work was within reach, and they believed that options existed that had not yet been in view. Melissa Dyrdahl said it was the same feeling she'd had in her twenties: "I feel the whole world is in front of me, I have all these choices, and I can do all these amazing things!"

While New Radicals are in this receptive state, we spend time talking about how the wake-up call has changed them. We engage in fascinating discussions about how such difficulties might even be good for us—as human beings, as New Radicals, and perhaps even for society as a whole. "What," I like to ask, "do you think the uses of adversity might be?" This delightfully wry phrase "the uses of adversity" isn't mine. Jonathan Haidt uses it in his book *The Happiness Hypothesis: Finding Modern Truth in Ancient Wisdom*. Haidt, an associate professor of psychology at the University of Virginia, writes that, "People need adversity, setbacks, and perhaps even trauma to reach the highest levels of strength, fulfillment, and personal development." In fact, he says, researchers have begun to move beyond studying how human beings cope with adversity to focus on the benefits of severe stress—sometimes called "post-traumatic growth." Haidt's findings mirror what I'm seeing with New Radicals. First, Haidt writes, in rising to the challenge, we reveal our hidden capabilities. This, in turn, changes our self-concept: we realize that we are much stronger than we once thought. Second, trauma "opens people's hearts and minds to one another," and relationships are strengthened as a result. Third, difficulties change our priorities and philosophies, leading "many people to consider changing careers." Story after story in this book will show how true this has been for the pioneers of this movement.

Now that we're aware and eager to get moving, what's next? Pretty much everybody wants to start *today*. But the truth is that few people step directly into a New Radical role. Even if they get a "bolt out of the blue" idea, there is still much to be done. For most New Radicals, three phases of research lie directly ahead. First, there is taking stock of what you have to offer. (What expertise and resources do you bring to the table?) Second, introspection is needed. (What really matters to you now?) And third, there's taking a look at the world around you. (What are the most pressing issues of our times, and how might you help?)

My clients and I also discuss how to prepare for the journey ahead. We talk about time. Creating a New Radical role takes time, which is always in short supply. New Radicals need to make room in their busy schedules—to think hard about what is on their plates, and what can be dropped, postponed, or delegated. Of course, it's not just about finding time in each day but also making a commitment to what can be a long journey. Depending on how extensive your transformation is—whether you will become mildly or wildly radical—the process can take months, and even years. Dr. Victoria Hale, the founder and CEO of the Institute for OneWorld Health, put it this way: "The timelines around these incredible adventures are not what you'd think. Don't underestimate how long it can take."

And we talk about support. Fast or slow, the New Radical journey can be challenging. On the early part of our voyage, we are likely to feel exhilarated, and this energy and enthusiasm will carry us a long way. But the road ahead also will be bumpy, there will be unexpected detours, and we simply may run out of gas, which is why, again and again, New Radicals discover the importance of others. "Our society is obsessed with individual accomplishment and self-sufficiency," Dan O'Brien, a rancher who is returning his American Great Plains spread to its original wild state, said. "We live in a world where asking for help can be seen as a sign of weakness. I am thankful for the people who've been with me on this journey."

One cautionary note: New Radicals soon discover that not everyone is thrilled about what they are doing. One of my clients told me outright that she wasn't going to inform her family and friends, whom she felt would encourage her to keep her high-paying job. Only her husband would know what she was planning. "If they knew, they'd only try to talk me out of it, and I can't cope with that right now. I have more than enough anxiety to go around!"

SERENDIPITY

My clients have also heard me say to "keep your eyes open and your senses on full alert!" Why? Because an extraordinary number of New Radicals have had unexpected encounters that have proven very useful. It makes sense that the more we are open to such experiences, the more likely we are to notice them. And if we notice them, we'll be prepared to take advantage of what they offer. If such talk makes you slightly uneasy, you're not alone. When reporting such fateful moments, New Radicals often are sheepish. They frame this part of their stories in ways that accord with their worldview, talking about things such as "coincidence," "chance encounter," and "being in the right place at the right time." However we explain it to ourselves, there is no doubt that synchronicity is at work. Consider the Aldermans, who happened to see a story on *Nightline* that gave them their first glimpse of their New Radical future. Epiphanies roused Scott Johnson and Nicole Pageau. And an article in the travel section sent Rocco Rossi on his second journey.

Sometimes, New Radicals interpret these moments as signals that they are on the right path. Mark Brayne is a prime example. Mark has successfully combined his first career—BBC foreign correspondent—with his second: he now helps journalists cope with the trauma they experience while on difficult assignments. Looking back, he could see that a series of coincidences kept him moving in a particular direction: "I remember going to a dinner party in London. I was heading into my midlife crisis and met someone at this party. 'What do you do?' I asked her. 'I'm a psychotherapist,' she replied. 'What's that?' said I." Here he laughed out loud at his naivety. "Astonishing, really, looking back. I had no idea, and yet she was precisely the right person for me to meet."

Paul Gillespie served with the Toronto Police Service for nearly 30 years, the last 6 as the officer in charge of the Child Exploitation Section of the Toronto Police Sex Crimes Unit. Paul is as tough and grounded as they come, but he, too, had a story. When it became clear that a database he'd been working on (more on Paul's story in Chapter 8) was going ahead and that he would be traveling the world to talk about it, he had a moment of doubt: "Who am I, this municipal policeman who has the audacity to tell smart people in Washington and London what to do?" It was Christmas, and he was heading into the liquor store to buy supplies for the family party. A Salvation Army volunteer was standing at the door, asking for donations. When Paul gave her the last of his change, she handed him a card whose message gave him the strength to carry on. "I opened it, and read a line from the Bible, something like 'no one can close the doors I have opened for you.' And that gave me the boost I needed. I felt that someone was helping me in my work."

I wondered if someone who has talked to thousands of executives moving between the for-profit and nonprofit sectors had heard similar things from his clients. "Yes!" was the emphatic one-word answer of David Simms, managing partner of the innovative placement firm Bridgestar. David says that, as a Christian, he feels that the Lord leads him, but that many of his firm's clients also talk about the phenomenon. "They use words like 'serendipity' to describe their experience of things falling into place."

On my own journey, the synchronicities were endless. My favorite example is as follows. One sultry summer afternoon, feeling anxious about whether my book and new business would ever get off the ground and at a loss for what to do with myself, I switched on the television. A BBC Wales documentary unfolded before my astonished eyes. It told the story of Hokusai, a Japanese artist and printmaker (1760–1849). Hokusai had a long and successful career and was looking forward to a comfortable retirement. At the age of 70, he was shocked to discover that his grandson had spent all of the money he had carefully saved. So Hokusai went back to work, creating what many art historians believe is his greatest body of work. Among these pieces is a print that secured his fame in Japan and around the world: the Great Wave. This particular piece seemed to me to be made for New Radicals: an enormous wave dominates the left side of the work, framing Mt. Fuji in the distance, and appears ready to engulf a small boat of fishermen. But the violence of the sea is balanced by the relaxed confidence of the expert fishermen, and although it depicts a storm, the sun is shining. Several months later, en route to my first official interview for this book, I walked by a shop and there, in the window, was a huge sheet of handmade wrapping paper, printed with Hokusai's Great Wave. I bought it and took it in a neat little roll into my new life, not missing the delicious simplicity of "roll" and "role" coming together in that moment.

A MOVEMENT FOR EVERYONE

Sometimes I'm asked if only certain people can become New Radicals. And my answer is that everyone can. This is *not* a movement just for elites—I've met people from all walks of life who are reinventing their work. New Radicals of all ages are appearing in every field, each sector, and around the world. And if one of the hallmarks of New Radicals—the ability to see things in a positive light—doesn't come naturally to you, there are lots of resources to help you shift. (We'll explore this idea in more detail throughout the book.)

That said, as New Radicals, we have an enormous privilege: the freedom to choose how we will make a living and how we will spend the rest of our lives. This certainly isn't the case for billions of people on this planet, which is why New Radicals take the next question seriously: "What do you have to offer?"

Chapter 3

What Do You Have to Offer?

Bees are dying in huge numbers. Colony collapse disorder has been reported in 35 U.S. states, and has spread to Canada and Europe. Estimates peg American beekeeper losses at about $150 million. And perhaps $15 billion worth of crops are at risk in the U.S. alone.

—*Los Angeles Times*, June 2007
Globe and Mail, June 2007

"You've got my attention, now what?" emerging New Radicals ask themselves.

It's a natural question, and my answer is to begin with an inventory of what we bring to the table: our experience and expertise. There are several good reasons to start at this point. The first is because New Radicals want to be fully engaged by their work. As Kevin Salwen of *Motto* magazine discovered at the end of his first career, using "10 to 15 percent of our brain" just isn't enough. As you'll see, making a comprehensive assessment of our abilities improves our chances of finding a role that is truly challenging.

A second reason is because New Radicals aren't just changing jobs, they are stepping off the traditional career trajectory altogether. They are applying what they have learned in the first half of their working lives to something new. And in order to do so, they must often detach these abilities from their original profession. They need to create what I think of as a portfolio of transferable skills.

A third reason to start with an inventory of experience and expertise is because we need to be able to articulate why we're the best person for the job. While it's easy to say—as I did in Chapter 1—that we now have "the expertise, knowledge, and resources to do what we once only dreamed of," making the case to others isn't necessarily a cakewalk. In fact, when I first started tracking this movement, New Radical pioneers were not always welcomed with open arms. When one seasoned leader approached an area hospital, she was offered a position as a candy striper.

ASSESSING YOUR SKILLS

There are a number of well-established tools to help people take stock (for instance, the Myers-Briggs Type Indicator is a great way to learn about our so-called soft skills). Sometimes, my clients and I make use of them. More often than not, though, we simply talk about the clients' careers, highlighting what they have learned, accomplished, and felt most proud of along the way. For instance, we talk about their most significant accomplishments, what they would imagine telling their twentysomething self about what they've learned, and what skills and abilities they want to carry forward into their new role. It's a fascinating and deeply rewarding exercise, and I highly recommend that you do it for yourself.

Sometimes we invite those in their immediate circle—colleagues, of course, but also family and friends—to weigh in with their observations and thoughts. It's gratifying when these findings line up—and even better when the external view matches the budding New Radical's sense of himself or herself.

While we're reviewing the past, we also talk about what might happen in the months and years to come. At midlife, people often think that they have already discovered everything there is to know about themselves. I urge my clients to recall Jonathan Haidt's research findings—that is, that "posttraumatic growth" can reveal our hidden capabilities. And I suggest that they stay open to what emerges and notice how they are changing.

It's fascinating to watch people get it, to really begin to see how they can use what they have learned to have a broader impact on the world. People say things to me like, "I realized I can apply what I've learned in building this business to something that actually makes a dent in the world's problems," "It's not about starting over, which I had feared, but becoming aware of what I do well," and "You get on a track and it's how you define yourself—who knew that, at 52, a bunch of new possibilities would open up for me?"

Consider the case of Sam Zimmerman. For many years, Sam was a transportation planner, working on some of North America's most successful public transit systems. Sam realized that he had a valuable skill set that could be brought to bear on the problems of the world's most congested and poorest cities. Today, he is an urban transport advisor to the World Bank, bringing a lifetime of experience to cities in the developing world. Hanoi is just one of more than a dozen cities he's helped to make more sustainable in the last few years. "In 2001, the only public transit were car and motorcycle taxis. Now, there are more than 700 buses in the city, and 750,000 daily riders."

While Sam was able to apply his skills to similar work, Tony Leighton discovered that his expertise was invaluable in a dramatically different role: "I was able to take my writing skills, my knowledge of marketing, and my grasp of technology—all of which came directly from my profession—and apply these to my newfound activism." (You'll read more about Tony in Chapter 8.)

And sometimes New Radicals have discovered that their first and second careers can work in tandem. As Mark Brayne told us in the last chapter, he had been a foreign correspondent for the British Broadcasting Corporation (BBC). When he first started studying psychology, all he could think about was getting out of journalism. But the farther he got down the new path, the more he recognized strong parallels with the old one. "One day I realized, hang on a moment, there are real overlaps here. Rather than running away from journalism, what I need to do is circle back in. In fact, I could bring things I was learning on the psychology track to bear on the practice and experience of journalism." As a consultant to news organizations, he is now sharing his thoughts on these overlaps with others. "The things therapists know about—attentive and respectful listening, context, setting boundaries, and so on—can help make journalists better at what they do, and enhance their emotional safety."

Jamie Kennedy, age 50, also merged long-standing and newly acquired abilities. But he did so without changing jobs. Jamie had secured his place as one of Canada's most celebrated chefs, and he could have continued to offer his patrons sublime creations in convivial surroundings well into his dotage. But he knew that there was something deeply crazy—and completely unsustainable—about the way restaurants source ingredients.

When we spoke by phone one cold winter's night, he outlined the challenge. Chefs face the same problems consumers do—there are something like 45,000 items in a typical grocery store, but few come from the local area. "Even in season, it's tough to find fruits and vegetables grown in southern Ontario. Instead, we buy broccoli grown on thousand-acre farms in California."

Jamie knew that remedying this long-standing problem was his first challenge and that helping to create a market for local farmers and producers wouldn't be an easy task: "Finding steady, dependable sources was a gradual and sometimes frustrating process." In the beginning, farmers simply couldn't keep pace with what chefs needed, nor could they be consistent with supply. Jamie responded by rethinking what his kitchen prepared: "Each day I would come up with a new menu, based on what was available."

Local ingredients were only part of the story—Jamie was interested in seasonal cuisine as well. But unlike Southern California, where local, seasonal cuisine was introduced in North America (thanks to people like Alice Waters and her innovative Chez Panisse), Canada has a short growing season. For Jamie, it was just another challenge to be met, and he hit upon the idea of taking a historic approach. "We would preserve things in the summer and feature them on the menu in the winter."

Curious to know how it works in practice, and since we were having this conversation in January, I asked him what was on the menu that evening. He put down the phone and dashed into the restaurant. When he returned, he described something that my grandmother might have made when I was growing up, though with a modern twist—and a chef's expertise: "Tonight, we have a pickled wild leek and winter greens salad. We harvested the leeks last spring, put them into a marinade and jarred them, and here they are nine months later. We also have roast heritage pork, which is produced by a guy in Grey County using a breed called Berkshire. That is served with braised red cabbage grown by a local organic farmer we've worked with for years. And an iced apple sauce—iced apple is like ice wine, but made from apples in Quebec."

His customers are pleased that Jamie's New Radical role continues to evolve. With local, seasonal cuisine well established as his signature style, he adds something to each new venture. "Each restaurant is a little further along in our thinking." For instance, at Jamie Kennedy at the Gardiner, they are serving only Ontario wines as part of their goal to establish a regional identity. "So that, when you eat here, it means as much as it would if you were in a particular part of France or Italy."

In 2008, Chef Kennedy is opening a third restaurant that will surpass everything he's done to date. The new establishment will be on his farm in Prince Edward County—a piece of pastoral paradise on Lake Ontario that is a burgeoning wine and artisanal foods region. "Everything we serve will be grown or produced within a 5-kilometer [3.1-mile] radius."

PLAYING TO YOUR STRENGTHS

The value of recognizing one's strengths isn't a new idea. But there is growing evidence that developing our strengths in the workplace (as opposed to fixing our flaws) is a smart thing to do, because it leads to employee satisfaction, greater productivity, and improved results.

While the definition of strengths is pretty simple—they are our natural talents—discovering them and figuring out how to put them into play is more complex. Dr. Martin Seligman, chairman of the University of Pennsylvania's Positive Psychology Center and founder of the emerging field of positive psychology (an umbrella term for the study of positive emotions and traits), has identified six human strengths that he says occur in virtually every culture around the world: wisdom, courage, humanity, justice, temperance, and transcendence.

oil field workers

What does this have to do with New Radicals? My clients and I talk about how understanding our strengths will ensure that they are called on in our New Radical role—we're taking the basic idea and applying it to our journey. Using our strengths will help generate more personal fulfillment—which is one-half of the New Radical promise. And because our chances of being more effective are greatly enhanced if our strengths are in play, our potential to make a significant difference also increases—the second half of the promise.

In a neat twist, one of the first books aimed at helping people in the workplace develop their strengths uses a New Radical pioneer as an example. *Now, Discover Your Strengths*, by Gallup researchers Marcus Buckingham and Donald O. Clifton, cites Warren Buffett as an example of someone who has built a career around his strengths. Buffett, they argue, parlayed patience into a unique investment perspective: only companies whose trajectory he could comfortably predict over the next two decades earned a place in his portfolio. (Both Gallup and Seligman have developed tools to help people identify their strengths—you'll find them listed in the Resources section at the back of this book.)

Focusing on what we're good at sounds like a great way to spend the rest of our lives, doesn't it? New Radicals like Suzanne Seggerman certainly think so. When Suzanne and I first crossed paths, I thought she was doing interesting New Radical work. But as we talked, it became clear that she is also a fine example of someone who considered her innate abilities when creating a new role for herself. She saw a need, but also knew that launching a new organization—Games for Change—would allow her to play to one of her key strengths: perspective. She could have continued to work for others—she was working with some pretty smart and interesting people—or she could have gone off and designed the games herself. "But I realized what I'm good at is thinking about the big picture, raising the visibility of serious games, and creating relationships that will help the industry develop. Starting Games for Change allowed me to do all that and more."

And then there is Dr. Mark Grabowsky. Mark, age 50, agreed to a conversation about his work "only because it will make my mother proud." And while I'm pleased to add to Mrs. Grabowsky's happiness, I chose Mark because he's one New Radical who made powerful use of his natural talents. In particular, Mark was able to use his ingenuity—a subset of wisdom in Seligman's classification—to great effect.

Like many New Radicals, Mark started out on a path that was predetermined. He came from a military family—his father, uncle, and brother were all graduates—so he headed off to the naval academy. Mark wanted to become a doctor, but a policy change meant that his dream was dashed. "While I was there, they changed the rules, and said no one in my class could become a physician."

In response, he quit and enrolled in a liberal arts college instead. As you might have guessed, this bump in the road was actually the beginning of his liberation. It was there that Mark began to learn more about what was really important to him: "Two things happened. First, in studying ethics, I was influenced by utilitarian values—that is, pursuing the greatest good for the greatest number as a working principle. And then I joined the Peace Corps."

While teaching in Kenya, he noticed that his students were often too ill to come to class. His utilitarian ideal came back to him, and he realized that helping them to improve their health would be a better way of ensuring their future, so back to med school he went. (Here, I imagined his mother heaving a sigh of relief.)

After finishing his medical training, Mark joined the public health service and has worked for the U.S. Centers for Disease Control (CDC) ever since. He has carved out a rewarding career, including a secondment to the American Institutes of Health, working on a vaccine for acquired immunodeficiency syndrome (AIDS). Through it all, he kept thinking about how measles was killing half a million kids each year in Africa, compared to none in the United States. "And all we had to do to save their lives was to vaccinate them."

And here we really begin to see Mark's signature strength in action. He jumped at the chance to work with the World Health Organization (WHO) and Red Cross in Uganda, developing strategies for measles control. They examined all the options—a mass campaign? vaccinate young people? old people? around outbreaks only?—and eventually decided on a strategy. "We would vaccinate everyone under 15 years of age, and then every three years vaccinate those born since the last campaign."

It was a huge success. Yet the next challenge lay immediately before them: how to apply the idea across the entire continent? At first, it wasn't at all clear how this enormous undertaking might be realized. But then Mark hit upon an approach that had never been tried before—he created a virtual organization: "We gathered a whole range of people that act over there—from foundations to U.N. agencies, from bilateral donors to health consultants and scientists—and we said, 'Each of you wants to work with us on this problem, and here is a structure that we can use to work together . . .'"

In retrospect, it sounds so simple, but this innovative solution was incredibly difficult to pull off. It's not easy to get international organizations to work together effectively—each has its own mandate, leadership, and politics. While the idea was ingenious, making it happen required logistical skill and considerable diplomacy, too. It worked because, by appealing to each organization's individual mission, they would only need a common goal to hold them all together. Mark laughed when he told me, "I called it a 'coalition of the willing' because it had no employees, no budget, and no bureaucratic layers."

Did they ever get results! More than 200 million kids were vaccinated, measles deaths decreased by 75 percent, and the entire effort was under target costs. Measles went from being the second or third leading cause of childhood death in Africa to being virtually eliminated. Here, one could be forgiven for thinking, "job well done, end of story." In fact, it was another beginning: while it was great to succeed with this initiative, they knew they had to keep moving. "How would we get new mothers back for shots if there had been no measles in their area?"

Incredibly, the best was yet to come. For so long, aid work had focused on the supply side of the equation. "You know, 'If you tell them, they will come.'" Mark said that it works well in the West, but not in Africa, where such thinking actually impoverishes the recipients: "If a woman comes to a clinic with her child, she doesn't get to spend that time doing whatever she needs to do to feed herself and her family. We have asked her to make a trade-off: come to the clinic and starve, or eat today."

Mark acknowledged that his time in the Peace Corps helped him to see this problem in a way that others could not: "Yes, for sure, I know what it's like to live without running water and electricity and to have to walk miles to catch a bus." But he also pointed out that good science is available: kids in inner-city Los Angeles weren't being vaccinated either. Researchers realized that mothers had to come in many times—sometimes 15 or 20 visits to a clinic—before their children got everything they needed. "That's what I'd call a heroic effort. And this helped shift our thinking in Africa." They would try something that had never been done before and use it to address one of Africa's most pressing issues.

Their target was malaria, a huge problem on the continent. The WHO estimates that it kills 1 million African children each year. Mark's team (by 2005, he was working with The Global Fund to Fight AIDS, Tuberculosis and Malaria to help implement these strategies) reasoned that if they offered mothers insecticide-treated bed nets, they would get their attention. And then, at the same time, they could give their kids measles shots, deworming pills, and Vitamin A. "It's known as 'integration,' and we're taking this new approach to as many communities as we can, so that they don't have to make the trade-off I talked about earlier."

In this campaign, Mark's strengths and utilitarian ideal came together in a way that he could not have imagined: "A local doctor told me that if we get rid of measles, he could close the measles ward. But that if we eliminate malaria, he could close the hospital."

WORKING TOGETHER IN NEW WAYS

As Mark Grabowsky's story illustrates so clearly, New Radicals are working together in new ways. We simply aren't limited by traditional approaches.

Why is this happening? I see two main influences. First, New Radicals are moving between sectors like never before—the largest migration, for instance, is executives from the corporate world moving to the not-for-profit sector—and cross-fertilization of ideas and practices is a natural by-product. The TED Conference is perhaps the best-known example of this unprecedented meeting of minds. TED stands for Technology, Entertainment, and Design, though its scope is much broader today. It's been called the U.S. alternative to the World Economic Forum in Switzerland, and was described in a May 14, 2007, *New Yorker* article by Michael Specter as "one of the few places on earth where you can see Bill Clinton, E. O. Wilson, or Philippe Starck chatting amiably with Kareem Abdul-Jabbar, Cameron Diaz, or Paul Simon."

Second, as a result of their wake-up call, New Radicals are open to new ideas and experiences. And, therefore, they are more inclined to come up with fresh solutions—as you have already seen, and will hear more about throughout this book. All of which is something our world sorely needs. And, lest you think I'm a voice in the wilderness on this, consider what Thomas Homer-Dixon, director of the Trudeau Centre for Peace and Conflict Studies and professor of political science at the University of Toronto, has to say on the matter.

In his new book, *The Upside of Down: Catastrophe, Creativity, and the Renewal of Civilization,* he argues that human beings can either choose our future or have it thrust upon us. He also identifies actions to take if we want to choose a positive path forward. One of these actions is to reduce the force of underlying stresses:

OPEN

Stresses

Choose

Thrust

Little Prince Antoine quote about future: — enable the future

> *Experts of all types have generated a considerable quantity of good ideas about how we can reduce the force of the tectonic stresses I've identified in this book—population imbalances, energy shortages, environmental damage, climate change, and income gaps. Yet too often the experts operate only within the silos of their disciplines and professional communities. Demographers don't want to talk to energy specialists, agronomists don't speak to economists, and climate scientists don't talk to epidemiologists. Instead, experts usually target the problems they understand, and because they don't think much about how to integrate their ideas with the ideas of experts focusing on related problems, the policies they propose are too narrowly focused. [p. 281]*

New Radicals are at ease moving between silos and even straddling disciplines in ways that traditionalists might frown upon. Ken Caldeira, once an information technology (IT) consultant on Wall Street, now a climate scientist at the Carnegie Institution—and a leading voice on ocean acidification and climate change—is a good example. He came to his new field later in life, so he brings a different perspective than the people who have worked in it all their lives. "I am the fox, running around looking into all kinds of things. That's a rarity in science—jumping around in a world that's all about deep expertise. I think I'm good at seeing the forest, and I know when to call in the people who've got the depth of expertise on particular trees that I don't have."

Some New Radicals simply break all the rules, ignoring protocol altogether. It's hard to think of a more audacious pioneer than

Dr. Craig Venter. After creating waves in the scientific community for his privately funded work on the human genome sequencing, this high school dropout has a new project underway. The Global Ocean Sampling Expedition aims to sequence the DNA of microorganisms in water samples collected around the world. Dr. Venter's first expedition tripled the number of proteins known to science, a huge bounty for biologists. The scientist says that biotechnology will also be able to make use of these findings, for example, by turning them into energy and useful chemicals.

And still other people, such as Bridgestar's David Simms, are building bridges between once disparate worlds. Bridgestar is the placement division within the Bridgespan Group consulting firm, whose goal is to bring talent from the for-profit world to the nonprofit sector. "We're bringing people with a whole bevy of skills—such as corporate executives—to mission-driven organizations where they can have a real impact."

One man personifies all the ideas in this chapter. When Scott Johnson and I exchanged stories one morning, I realized that the organization he founded, the Myelin Repair Foundation (MRF), brings people together in unexpected ways and is breaking new ground as a result. And his New Radical role allows him to put his skills and strengths into play. "It was as though everything I had done so far prepared me to step into this new position." Scott's first career had four pillars that would help in his second one: his initial training as an engineer, which is all about problem solving and being very logical; his background in strategic consulting, concerned with how big companies should face the future and what they need to do differently; his experience inside a large corporation, which would be useful because

MRF would interface with biotech companies and understanding their culture and how they work would be important; and, finally, his start-up experience, so he was comfortable launching something new. "Not only would I have ideas, but I'd be able to execute them."

Multiple sclerosis was a particularly powerful motivator for Scott. Now 51, he was diagnosed with the disease when he was 20. Living with it for more than three decades, he realized that an effective treatment, much less a cure, wasn't likely in his lifetime. A tiny article about myelin repair in a business magazine was enough to capture Scott's imagination. He began looking into myelin repair research, trying to understand what was going on.

It may have begun as a personal journey, but it didn't stay that way for long. What really got him hooked was when he started talking to people in medical research and realized that the current system wasn't working. "If you were to design a system that was the least efficient in actually coming up with treatments to help people with diseases, you would come up with what's currently done." At this, my eyebrows shot up, and I said that this statement sounded, well, counterintuitive. In fact, there are three clear reasons for Scott's bold assertion.

First, at American universities, scientists get grants from either the largest funder of academic research—the National Institutes of Health—or needs foundations such as the American Cancer Society. The problem is that academic scientists are rewarded for publishing, and this arrangement discourages them from divulging information until it appears in print. By the time a scientist has an idea for an experiment, applies for and receives funding, does the experiment, writes up the paper, and—assuming it is successful—finally gets the paper reviewed by peers and published, four to six years can have elapsed. "That's a huge time lag when someone else could have taken this new learning and built on it. And yet that is the way the world works."

The second thing is that grant applications are reviewed by peers. A group of scientists evaluates the quality of the science before it gets the nod for funding. This arrangement sets them up to do incremental experiments so that they are sure to receive the resources they need. "Which means that really brilliant scientists often don't put their best ideas out there." And the third thing is that disease has gotten very complicated. The easier insights were unearthed in the last one hundred years, and now things are complex and require deep expertise. "Collaboration is urgently needed, but there just isn't a mechanism that allows it, much less encourages it."

So, what Scott set out to do amounts to nothing short of shaking up the world of medical research. In launching the foundation, his first task was to assemble the best team possible—a group of scientists who could help him take on the challenge of figuring out how to do research more effectively and accelerate research into myelin repair treatments. Five of the world's leading neuroscientists—each of whom approaches the study of myelin from a different perspective (immunology, genetics, developmental biology, molecular biology, and proteomics)—joined the team.

How is their approach different, and how well is it working? Their Accelerated Research Collaboration™—or ARC™—is based on three elements: collaboration, acceleration, and results. Collaboration means that the team works together on an outcome-driven research plan. Acceleration means that they have identified 13 new myelin repair drug targets and more than a dozen new research tools. And results: they have an aggressive intellectual property protection program that allows them to engage with pharmaceutical companies and license discoveries for further development and clinical trials. (This final point, they believe, will finance the organization in the long run.) "In short, we've developed a unique hybrid model that is cutting the time to drug discovery in half."

But the best part, Scott confided to me, is that other disease organizations have come calling. The ARC model can be applied to any medical research problem once basic, relevant scientific discoveries have been made. The American Cancer Society and 50 other medical charities have inquired about ARC's radically new approach. "The work itself is stimulating to everyone on our team. But the fact that we have this validation from other disease organizations makes us realize that we are on the right track. It sounds kind of hokey, but we think we're going to change the world."

YOUR RESOURCES AT WORK

As I worked with emerging New Radicals and interviewed the pioneers, I realized that skills and strengths were only part of the picture. Capacity was important, but something more fundamental, something deeper, was at work. I discovered a common thread running through all of the stories and recognized that this quality might be the most important of all. We have often heard it said that people are an organization's most important asset—in fact, the *right* people are. My research leads me to believe that one's character—the kind of person you are—has more weight than educational background, practical skills, specialized knowledge, or work experience. "Each of those things can be acquired," Ken Caldeira rightly pointed out.

Stephen Lewis, the former U.N. special envoy for HIV [human immunodeficiency virus]/AIDS in Africa, says something that indicates that he holds a similar view. Young people often approach him after he speaks and ask what courses they should take so that they can do good works. "I smile to myself and then tell them that I wouldn't be so presumptuous as to offer advice. But I do share my single experience with hiring lots of people, which was when I was with UNICEF [United Nations Children's Fund] in New York. I discovered that it wasn't particular skills that we were looking for at all. That what we realized we really needed were decent human beings who truly care and who are willing to devote themselves to this work." The kind of people Stephen is talking about—whom you'll encounter throughout this book—will do everything in their power to make a difference, to achieve a mission. They simply can't imagine doing anything less.

THE CASE FOR CONTINUING

At this stage, New Radicals-in-the-making are feeling pretty good. They have taken stock of what they have learned and accomplished, and they understand their strengths. It's been a good way to get them back on their feet after the unsettling wake-up call. And it's healthy to spend time in appreciation of first careers. At this point, many clients of mine announce that they are now ready to select a New Radical role for themselves. Sometimes, in fact, they do. For the most part, though, there is still work to be done. And here's why: People who go after a New Radical position at this stage tend to choose one that is easy to see or within comfortable reach. Yet I've found that if clients stay open to the possibilities along the continuum a little longer, they are more likely to discover a role that is ideal. That getting to know themselves a little better and focusing on how, precisely, they might make a difference lead to work that offers maximum personal satisfaction.

Now that we've got our sea legs, it's time to head into deeper waters—to learn a little more about what's going on inside of us, by answering the question, "What moves you?"

Chapter 4

What Moves You?

A tidal wave of migrants is swamping Europe, with Malta as the latest point of entry. Most of these desperate human beings come from the horn of Africa, leaving Libya on over-crowded, un-seaworthy vessels. Some die en route, but many more reach the island nation—equivalent to half the country's birthrate each year.

—*The Economist*, June 2007

Karen Bookstore
CNC
& offer to do
MABTT

Most of us don't have a deep sense of who we are & what we value our inner self

anesthetized to real self

what really matters quote

Look too closely = pain Newman quote

know self be self or pain

Who are you? Now that we've assessed what you do, it's time to answer this more fundamental question: who's underneath the polished exterior? We need to find the answer because, as New Radicals, we want our work to reflect our values, and having more insight into our deeper, more authentic selves improves our chances of success.

You may already have the answer to the question of who you are. Most of us don't, however. And there are many reasons for our lack of knowledge. Being busy comes at the top of most everyone's list. We have worked hard to carve ourselves into a particular shape, such as lawyer, parent, spouse. This identity has served us well, but it also means that we don't have enough time to do everything on our list, much less make friends with our inner self. Over time, we've become anesthetized to our real selves. Our vision has blurred, and we've lost sight of our dreams. It's not surprising, given that ours is a world that doesn't value or reward the inner life, which is why my clients sometimes refuse to do this part of the process, or they find reasons to bail out at this point. They may not be interested in or see the importance of their deepest self, or they may simply be wary. I tell them that it's possible to become a New Radical without doing a deep dive, but I ask them to consider two points before skipping ahead or dropping out. One reason, I reassure them, is that what we're about to do is not really so mysterious. We're simply taking a break from the incessant chatter of our conscious minds and creating a welcoming environment for fresh insights. If you have ever had the solution to a vexing problem come to you when you were doing something else, you have experienced what I'm talking about. (British scientists call it the 3Bs: they say that great discoveries are made on the bus, in the bath, or in bed.) The second reason to consider continuing is that people who do answer the question "What moves you?" report that it enriches their lives. As I tell my clients, "The choice is yours."

The wake-up call you—and other New Radicals-in-the-making—experienced helped launch the process of reconnecting with your deepest self. Now it's time to invest in a period of self-discovery, reaching inside and learning more about what touches us deeply and what matters most. Exploring this inner terrain is a highly personal process. When doing the assessments mentioned in Chapter 3, we were on common ground. Here, that's not the case. After all, we even have different ways of describing this deep self—everything from psyche to soul. Yet despite our differences, we share the challenge of creating the conditions that will allow us to explore ourselves.

How do New Radicals "turn on, tune in, and drop out," as Timothy Leary famously put it? Here are the two most popular routes. You'll notice immediately that they share a paradox: that in order to find ourselves, we must first lose ourselves. Willpower is *not* what you need (that's the conscious mind in action). In fact, "just un-do it" might be an appropriate slogan for this point on our journey.

GETTING LOST

Many New Radicals discover that taking a break from their busy lives—literally going away—is just what they need. Rocco Rossi, who we heard from earlier, took three such trips—one in the aftermath of his wake-up call, and two more along the Camino Frances in Spain. With each voyage, his understanding of what mattered and his ideas for a new role grew deeper and stronger.

If finding time in your schedule is a concern, I offer Ron Dembo as an alternative. Ron was running a company with offices around the world when the desire to change his life first seized him. He knew he was passionate about the environment, but he had no idea what he might do. But he *did* know how to find out: "Whenever I have to make big decisions, I go away somewhere really quiet—like the mountains, or a beach—where I can completely unplug. Even a few days give me the time and space to reflect on what's important to me, and what I might do next."

And Melissa Dyrdahl falls somewhere between the two. Once a senior vice president at Adobe, Melissa knew it was essential to find a place where no one knew her, where she could be herself and speak freely. She went on a retreat with six midlife women, all of them in transition, and each with a totally different story. Listening to them made her feel less alone, and the retreat gave her the safety and space to explore herself. "None of these women had a preconceived idea of who I was. And what happened is that I started to get connected with some parts of myself that I had ignored, pushed to the background, locked in a closet. As someone who had 500 people reporting to me, I was used to having all the answers. This time, I had none, but I trusted they would come. If I could just stay quiet and let it bubble to the surface."

GETTING LOST IN THE MOMENT

Other New Radicals found ways to be introspective without leaving the comforts of home. For instance, many of them keep journals. In fact, I give one to each of my clients as we begin to work together. I encourage them to keep track of things they notice—anything that catches their eye—as well as unexpected encounters, thoughts, and dreams. Glimpses of what moves you and new ideas may occur at unexpected moments—perhaps in that delicious time just before you fall asleep, or on waking. All of these things may provide insights we can use. Other clients say they want to sidestep language altogether, so we explore alternatives such as the arts—painting, dancing, or music. One client said he'd read something about how Keith Richards responds whenever he feels inspired: he yells "incoming!" and grabs a guitar. It makes a great story, but I want to underline that we are *all* creative. The arts can be, in Euclid's phrase, a "royal road" like no other.

Meditation is another great way to calm our minds. I often recommend Jon Kabat-Zinn's books to my clients. Kabat-Zinn is the founder and former director of the Stress Reduction Clinic and Center for Mindfulness in Medicine, Health Care, and Society at the University of Massachusetts Medical School, and he has written a number of books (see the Resources). Why is Kabat-Zinn recommended over other teachers? Because he has demystified meditation and taken it out of the realm of religion. Meditation, he says, is simply sitting, breathing in and out, and being present: "All that is required is a willingness to look deeply at one's present moments, no matter what they hold, in a spirit of generosity, kindness toward oneself, and openness toward what might be possible."

Once they've established a connection, New Radicals begin to see themselves through fresh eyes. As they do, they look for clues that might begin to reveal their new role—including their childhood dreams, their values, and what makes their hearts sing.

ACHIEVING YOUR CHILDHOOD DREAMS

What did you want to be when you grew up? Some New Radicals told me that a powerful dream had been with them since childhood. Its pent-up energy had propelled them into their new lives.

One New Radical dad, Don Stannard-Friel, wanted to tell me about an "aha!" moment he'd had with his son, Sean Stannard-Stockton. Sean, a philanthropic advisor, was working with Don's class of university students, helping them to learn more about giving. Listening to his son, Don realized that Sean's path had been evident since he was a little boy. "He had these hippie parents who didn't have a clue about money, and yet told us that wealthy people should give their money to good causes. And now that's just what he does—helps people figure out how their wealth can have a bigger social impact."

In contrast, David Chamberlain was deeply influenced by his grandparents. When he was just seven, he traveled with them to Haiti. His granddad was adamant that they not spend their holiday lounging poolside at some American-style hotel. Instead, he insisted that they take a taxi into the countryside where the real people lived. More than three decades later, David's memory of one particular morning is as clear as a bell: "We arrived at a rural marketplace and, as soon as the dust settled, everyone came out to look at us. After we passed inspection, a soccer ball flew in the air, and my perfectly dressed little self got caught up in a game with some of the poorest children on earth. We had a real connection with them that afternoon." That cross-cultural event came back to him time and again, and it would determine how he reinvented his adult self. After years in IT and the traditional tourism business, David now runs Exquisite Safaris. His company designs customized trips for people who want both to explore the world and to contribute to a community's needs at the same time.

Sometimes the connection between childhood and their new life took New Radicals by surprise. When Ken Caldeira, who left the IT sector to become a climate-change scientist, and I were talking about his new work, I asked him what he wanted to be when he was a little boy. "I grew up in the Apollo space program era. When I was six, if you'd asked me what I wanted to be when I grew up, I would have said a scientist." He paused as though considering the idea for the first time before reflecting: "I guess you could say I fulfilled a boyhood ambition."

For the fortunate few, the bond to one's inner child remains strong, even if the full realization of the dream took many years. That's certainly true for Dan O'Brien, age 59, a rancher on the Great Plains of the American West. When a mutual friend called to suggest that I interview Dan, I listened politely, thinking, "Rancher? New Radicals are urban professionals!" But the longer I listened, the more I realized that Dan's story had all the signatures of this movement. Clearly, I was going to find examples beyond the major cities of the world.

Dan and I started by talking about when his dream began. "We were on a family driving holiday. I was just a kid, sitting in the backseat, looking out at the land stretching north for thousands of miles into Canada, and I said to my mother, 'There, right there, where the land begins to flatten out, and the trees disappear, that's where I want to live.'"

I soon understood that Dan had started his "career" just as you and I did: by following in the footsteps of thousands before him. As a young man, he moved to South Dakota, bought the biggest piece of property he could afford, and became a cattle rancher. Like a long line of Great Plains farmers, he bought progressively larger pieces of land, battling drought, overgrazed pastures, falling cattle prices, and rising costs. It's not an easy life. To survive lean times, Dan took work for pay. Sometimes he'd work as a handyman, sometimes as a teacher. On occasion, Dan remembers, this supplementary work was deeply rewarding: "The best job of all was working on the reintroduction of the peregrine falcon to the west. It's an environmental success story, and I take great pride in having played a part in it." But each time, the goal was the same: to send money back to pay the mortgage and the ever-escalating debt on his beloved—and aptly named—Broken Heart Ranch.

Two things nudged him from this way of life and onto a New Radical path. The first was his growing awareness that the entire enterprise was built on a questionable foundation—as he puts it, "Raising cattle in semiarid grasslands that we keep trying to turn into Belgium." The second was the cumulative stress of such a life, compounded by a divorce. Dan describes it as "a series of financial and spiritual crises." He had reached his Waterloo.

After his classic New Radical wake-up, and as he was licking his wounds, Dan got a call from a friend—"out of the blue"—

inviting him to an annual buffalo roundup. He drove out onto the prairie, happy for a diversion from his problems, and wandered into a new world. As soon as he saw the buffalo, he knew that he had found his bliss and discovered what he would do with the rest of his life. "It was in coming face-to-face with these mammoth creatures that my passion for the Great Plains was reawakened. I knew in an instant that I would convert my ranch from cattle to buffalo—and, in doing so, help restore the plains to their original grandeur."

We talked about how his dream took shape. How it called on everything he'd learned up to that point and required him to get really clear about what was important to him at this time of his life. We also spoke about all the thinking, planning, and financial investment—not to mention hard work—that went into making this new way of living on the land possible.

With all of this before him, what Dan did first made me smile: he launched into a series of autodidactic lessons on wildlife ecology. Clearly this is a man who is passionately in love with this place and eager to absorb everything it had to teach him. "I began to educate myself about the flora and fauna that have had billions of years to perfect a strategy of survival." I was eager to learn, too: I wanted to know how the buffalo fit into this natural environment." He spoke poetically about the prairies: "Julia, two hundred years ago, they stretched unbroken across the continent. From Texas to Alberta, the Great Plains were as wild as the Serengeti, with huge herds moving constantly in all directions. And buffalo are the signature species of the plains: as ruminants, they prevent trees and shrubs from taking root, they spread grass seed as they move around and plant it with their hooves. And, of course, they are repaid with plenty of grass for lunch." We laughed.

As his lessons were progressing, Dan began to plan how he would convert his ranch, removing interior fences so that his new herd could roam freely, and reinforcing the exterior ones so that they could contain bigger, stronger animals. He told me that he started with 13 buffalo calves—"short-necked golden balls of wool"—and increased his herd to 75 within the year. But he also thought about how he would do things differently. He wasn't going to raise them as bigger, woollier cattle.

His new enterprise differs from cattle ranching in several important ways. First, he and his partners have set up a company to sell buffalo meat directly to consumers. They say it's the healthiest protein going—"lower in fat and calories than beef"—and needs to be marketed differently, too. This is why they are using the wine model and emphasizing difference rather than similarity. "The cattle model aims to produce T-bones that are indistinguishable from one another, no matter where you are. Following the wine model, I figured that a buffalo raised on the open prairie on native wheatgrass, plus whatever other species were abundant that year, should be as unique as a Cabernet from Napa Valley."

And there's another element of his strategy that is unique—something he calls the "humane harvest" of the buffalo. For Dan, how they die is as important as how they live: "I wanted them to be killed in the pasture as they would have been when the Sioux controlled these lands." He and a sharpshooter head out into the grasslands where the herd is, and shoot what they need. "The first time we did it, I expected the others to run, but not a single animal moved. It was over in seconds. And we bled them right there on the prairie, returning the buffalo's blood to the soil."

Before we ended our conversation, Dan said something that spoke volumes about his New Radical nature and made it abundantly clear that his boyhood dream had come true. He mentioned that as he was driving the first buffalo into town to be butchered and prepared for shipping, he pulled over to the side of the highway to do something he'd meant to do after they were killed, but got too caught up in the busyness of the moment to remember. "I burned some sweetgrass and waved it over them. I'm sure that people in their cars whizzing past wondered what I was doing. It had been a long time since someone had thanked a buffalo for its life."

LIVING BY YOUR VALUES

"We tell ourselves stories in order to live," says American essayist Joan Didion. We all grow up with guiding principles. Some people can cite their culture's values chapter and verse. Others tell me things like, "As my dad always said . . ." My clients and I bring these belief systems into the light of day, explore them, and determine together whether they are still—in whole or in part—appropriate for their emerging New Radical self. And I remind them about Jonathan Haidt's thoughts on posttraumatic growth—how difficulties can change our priorities and philosophies.

"The whispered longings of my heart"—that's how one client tearfully expressed what was going on inside of her as she began to extricate herself from a particularly powerful but outmoded set of guiding principles. To help her to see that she was not alone in searching for something more soulful and appropriate to her emerging self, I shared a Matthew Fox story. Fox, once a Roman Catholic priest (he was silenced by the Vatican in 1989 for his radical—or New Radical?—views), is now an Episcopal priest and prolific author. Fox talked about when he and a biophysicist performed a ritual on the sacredness of the body for a group of physicians. One at a time, the biophysicist showed an image of the body's 22 internal organs. One at a time, she spoke about how each organ serves us. After each presentation, the entire group bowed to the image, and chanted a thank you. When it was over, there was deep silence in the room. Never before had these professionals considered the body in quite this way.

"What might your new values be?" I ask my clients. "And how can you incorporate them into the role you hope to create?" Think about Rocco Rossi, and how after his first pilgrimage he began to wake up to what was important to him. He knew that he would have to find an organization that was in alignment with his emerging self.

Or consider Kye Marshall, age 63, who created an innovative professional practice that expresses who she is and helps others to do the same.

Kye and I sat down to talk in a cozy room filled with musical instruments of every description. As we spoke about her life and the new role she had created, I found myself wondering how many of us actually *know* what's most important to us when we're young. How can we know, when we are only beginning to discover ourselves and the world around us? The very best we can hope for is to find work that makes use of our interests and abilities.

This is precisely what Kye did. For 17 years, she was principal cellist for several important Canadian orchestras, including the O'Keefe Centre. But somewhere along the line, the work lost its allure, and Kye found herself feeling bored and restless. "Most people think playing in an orchestra is glamorous, but for me it really wasn't. It felt completely uncreative." While the desire for more creativity was growing in her, Kye was also stepping into New Radical territory: she was longing for more meaningful work. "I began to think about what I might do to make a difference in the world." And though she had no real sense about how to do that, she was quite clear that her contribution should be directly linked to her music. "I realized, what good would it do for me to go to Botswana to dig wells? I'm a trained musician! Wasn't there some way I could use my skills to help?"

Entering psychotherapy at this point in her life helped bring this desire to do good to the surface, as well as providing her with her first glimpse of the future. The process was insightful and healing, and she wondered if, in fact, *this* might become the way she would help others. "I realized this can really help people. Maybe I could become a psychotherapist."

Kye's story is a great example of how each New Radical's path is unique. While this book follows the standard course, few journeys, personal or otherwise, are linear. Instead of traveling "as the crow flies," some New Radicals move backward and forward through the stages until their new role comes into view. In Kye's case, she pursued a number of avenues simultaneously. She enrolled in an experiential psychology training course and, at the same time, completed a master's degree in psychology and counseling. Her transformation took place over several years, as she juggled courses and continued to develop as a musician—composing jazz and acquiring improvisation skills. To support herself, she turned to her first love, classical music. "I played freelance cello gigs for orchestras and private functions." One day, it occurred to her that she could combine it all—her classical training, her new skills in composition and improv, and her degree—in a single practice: "I decided to become a psychotherapist using music as a primary tool."

As we sat in her office, Kye and I talked about how this differs from traditional psychotherapy. In a nutshell, her clients use music to express what's going on inside of them. "Music is a form of communication that can help us access our inner world—particularly our emotions and feelings—and can reach defended, nonverbal parts of our psyche, too." In other words, music gives us a way to experience and understand our inner life in a way that words simply can't. I looked around at all the instruments—a piano, xylophones, dozens of drums and rattles, chimes, some string and wind instruments—and wondered aloud if all of her clients are professional musicians. "Oh, no! These aren't trained players. Most of them have never studied music or picked up an instrument in their lives." In a typical session, clients choose an instrument—or instruments—and play on a theme that came up in conversation. "We improvise, or create soundscapes together."

Improvisation is a vitally important part of Kye's unique approach to therapy, working on a number of levels for both client and therapist. One group she works with—women with eating disorders—is a vivid example of how transformative music can be. "When we play together, these women create something beautiful out of feelings they might experience as negative or ugly." And the instruments can also be safe vehicles for such feelings. "The instrument is angry, not me," is how Kye put it. And the third advantage for clients is that playing together gives them a sense of what's known in psychology as "agency": they can make something happen. "You've picked up an instrument, made a sound, and contributed to the creation of a piece of music."

The advantages of improvisation for the therapist include a much deeper and more constant connection to the client. "I can attune with my client almost continuously—I am in the process with them. We are in the music making together." As we discussed this topic and got deeper into our conversation about her new work, the face of the woman before me grew more animated. It was clear evidence of one of the best parts of becoming a New Radical—our work helps others, which makes it deeply rewarding for us.

One-on-one sessions are easy to picture, but what is it like when a big group plays together? It sounds like a recipe for cacophony, but, in fact, it's just the opposite. Somehow, the players become attuned to one another. "It's quite something to experience—a group of people, nonmusicians, playing together, making it up as we go along, not a word between us. Suddenly, we'll all speed up, or stop cold. No score. No conductor. Just human beings making music together. We look at each other with wide eyes and say 'Wow!'"

Kye also records these sessions. She and her clients talk about what the experience was like, and then they listen to the playback together. "It gives them a chance to hear—from the outside—an aural portrait of their inner life."

MAKING YOUR HEART SING

New Radicals aren't the first to look for satisfaction from their careers—the study of how to be happy at work is an ancient path stretching back as far as Aristotle, who said, "Where your talents and the needs of the world cross, there lies your vocation." In my practice, I use two modern-day gurus to help budding New Radicals move closer to their goal.

The first, of course, is Joseph Campbell. Campbell taught for many years at Sarah Lawrence College and had a lifelong interest in mythology. After Bill Moyers' series of interviews with Campbell aired on the American television network PBS in the 1980s (and many times since), his notion to "follow your bliss" became a catch phrase for our generation. Moyers asked a question: "Do you ever have the sense of being helped by hidden hands?" To which Campbell replied: "All the time. It is miraculous. I even have a superstition that has grown on me as a result of invisible hands coming all the time. Namely, that if you do follow your bliss, you put yourself on a kind of track that has been there all the while, waiting for you, and the life that you ought to be living is the one you are living. When you can see that, you begin to meet people who are in your field of bliss, and they open doors to you. I say, follow your bliss, and don't be afraid, and doors will open where you didn't know they were going to be."

Some of you will wave your hand and dismiss this thinking as a cliché. To which I reply, fair enough, but clichés always begin in truth. Bliss is an important clue. And while it may have been the baby boomers' mantra, many of us didn't quite achieve it. As New Radicals, we have a second chance.

One man gave us "bliss," and another gave us "flow." For decades, Mihaly Csikszentmihalyi, professor and former chairman of the Department of Psychology at the University of Chicago, has been studying states of what he calls "optimal experience." He coined the term "flow" to describe "total immersion in a task that is challenging yet closely matched to one's ambitions." Csikszentmihalyi also wanted to understand the role flow plays in life as a whole. So he studied successful creative people who built their lives around a consuming passion. He observed a wide range, including painters and dancers, physicists and biologists, novelists and psychologists. He discovered that, through an initial interest, his subjects developed relationships to people, practices, and values that deepened over the years, and both the frequency and duration of flow experiences increased as a result. Csikszentmihalyi called this "vital engagement: a relationship to the world that is characterized by both an experience of flow (enjoyed absorption) and meaning (subjective significance)."

What does this signify for New Radicals? In Csikszentmihalyi's work, we can discover cues that will help us move forward—by noticing when we experience flow. He also provides a glimpse of what the future holds in store for us: the promise of vital engagement.

One of my clients, a successful CPA eager to explore new options, had a hard time with this concept of flow. Although he could identify with being challenged by his work, and losing track of time, he felt that he was missing out on passion and joy. One day, I answered the phone to hear his excited eureka. He had taken up fishing with his youngest son, something he hadn't done since he was a boy. "I felt it, Julia," he told me breathlessly. "There, in that river up to my knees, I finally understood what it is to feel flow." I laughed with delight at the aptness of the metaphor and could feel him grinning at the other end of the phone line as it sunk in for him, too. Today, we are busy incorporating this feeling into his plans for the future.

Psychotherapist Mark Brayne was able to acknowledge flow in his life and even, in time, to recognize the hints it offered about his future. Working for many years as a foreign correspondent, he was always learning new languages—something he thoroughly enjoyed. "I began to see it was partly because I desperately wanted to communicate. In psychological terms I was looking for a way to understand myself. And, of course, that led me to two professions that are all about understanding others."

Melissa Dyrdahl used her experience of bliss in an equally prescient way. In addition to marketing at Adobe, she was responsible for corporate philanthropy, and while that task took up only 5 to 10 percent of her time, it resulted in 90 percent of her satisfaction. "It felt great to make decisions and influence how Adobe's success could have a real impact on organizations and people in our communities, through grants and software donation. That was a pretty powerful signal about what I wanted to do."

Johann Koss, age 38, knows something about being in the zone. A four-time Olympic Gold medalist in speed skating, he made world headlines when he won three gold medals for Norway at the 1994 Lillehammer games. When I caught up with him, he was packing for a trip to Africa. Before we began to talk about his new role, he wanted to impress on me how important sport has been in his life: "My life lessons came from my Olympic training. The importance of teams—even if you're competing as an individual. The importance of setting goals and finding ways to overcome obstacles. Plus, sport is the source of my emotional well-being—being active keeps me happy."

Immediately after the Olympics, Johann began to explore ways to do something meaningful with his life. Save the Children Norway sent him to Eritrea, which reinforced his desire to help children in need. When he first encountered young people who had, as he described it, "no chance to play," he was stunned, and the seed for his New Radical role was planted. "Children need play for their physical, psychological, and social development. I was meeting children who had no chance to play, none at all. But at the same time, their eagerness and readiness to do so was enormous."

Johann is now CEO of Right to Play. It's an organization that does much more than reintroduce disadvantaged kids to the joys of childhood. They focus on four key program areas: basic education, health promotion and disease prevention, conflict resolution and peace education, and community development.

Johann's team quickly discovered that these children needed to learn basic life skills—such as how to protect themselves from the diseases that are rampant in developing countries, including malaria and HIV—and that games were an ideal way to help. The vaccination game is a perfect example. "A group of kids stand in a circle, holding hands. One child stands inside the circle, and another tries to break through to tag him, which is pretty easy to do. Then we have the children form two circles, one outside the other—we talk about the outside one being the vaccination—and they immediately discover it's much harder to get through. A second circle improves your strength, you see. Your immune system."

Right to Play's life-saving role has many dimensions. In the refugee camps where the group often works, life is very different from what it might have been in villages or rural areas. "There is no normal," is how Johann put it. When his organization sets up a center with games for young children and organized sport for the older kids, a powerful shift happens. Young people respond to both the attention and the routine, and they begin to feel that they matter—that they belong. It's important for all of them, but particularly valuable for high-risk teenaged boys. It means that when soldiers come calling, they can resist. "They don't want to become child soldiers. They want to stay with us."

Johann doesn't tell me this, but I know that he donated the prize money from his 1,500-meter victory to this work, and he challenged other athletes around the world to do the same. And more than 300 Olympic and professional athletes from 40 countries have responded. They go into the field and—as ambassadors—raise awareness and funds. In doing so, they discover what Johann did: that it's an ideal fit. "They're highly motivated. They've been positively impacted by sport, and many of them are parents now. They know the difference play can make in a child's life."

Active is just the right word to describe Right to Play's involvement in more than 20 countries, including Azerbaijan, Benin, Chad, China, Ethiopia, Ghana, Indonesia, Jordan, Lebanon, Liberia, Mali, Mozambique, Pakistan, Palestinian Territories, Rwanda, Sierra Leone, Sri Lanka, Sudan, Tanzania, Thailand, Uganda, United Arab Emirates, and Zambia. Today, as they deepen their work in these nations, they are also turning their attention in an unexpected direction: toward the first world. They want to help Western youth get into shape. "We intend to promote sport and play in our own communities, where we are seeing an epidemic of obesity."

A THIRD KIND OF INTELLIGENCE

As I listened to people's stories—and read accounts of hundreds of others—I began to observe a common theme. Seligman had certainly struck a chord in shifting our thinking toward the positive. But it seemed to me that New Radicals were taking things a step further. New Radicals believe in the pull of vision. They recognize the power of dialogue. And New Radicals see the possibilities inherent in working together toward change. Yes, we are positive. We are also constructive and hopeful. In fact, I began to think of "positive, constructive, hopeful" as the New Radical credo. And this isn't just a neat phrase, but a tool we can actually use—a reference point for all of our choices and actions. "Try this experiment," I suggest to my clients. "The next time you need to make a decision, or when you're in a meeting and it's your turn to speak, run it through the 'positive, constructive, hopeful' filter first. I guarantee something will shift. And you'll begin to see that we change ourselves and influence others even in the simplest ways. Forget the world stage; right in the middle of daily life, you can make a difference."

All of this musing about a New Radical credo made me wonder if there isn't a growing desire for a moral code. I thought of Dr. Mark Grabowsky's utilitarian ideal. What came to mind, too, was something Bill Gates wrote in an op-ed piece in the *Wall Street Journal* about his work with their foundation: "This would do more than challenge our intellect. This would challenge our humanity."

At that point in my thinking, Dr. Robert Coles appeared on my radar for the first time in many years. Coles, a child psychiatrist and one of the best-known civil rights activists of the '60s, has spent a lifetime studying morality: what it is, how it's created, and its place in our lives. And now he's describing it as a third kind of intelligence. Coles says that we have known for a long time about rational or cognitive intelligence, and we have learned a lot in the last decade or so about emotional intelligence. But he claims that a third kind of intelligence—moral—is just as important, and people want more of it in their lives. And that sounds distinctly New Radical to me.

Coles, I was glad to learn, remains optimistic about our world. What's more, he believes that being hopeful about the future is our moral obligation. And he takes the things he's seen in his lifetime—including civil rights—as evidence that more positive change is possible.

MOVING ALONG THE PATH

At this point on their journey, New Radicals look to me like kindergarten students, as they wiggle excitedly on my couch, doing their best to sit still. They talk animatedly about letting go of the work they have been defined by and following their hearts. Melissa Dyrdahl described what so many are feeling at this point:

"It was hard for me to sit in meetings about how we were going to sell more software—were they going to buy $1.4 million or $1.6 million?—when what I really wanted to do was help some of the charities I'd been coming across do their work. How could I find a way to participate at a level where people don't even *have* a computer, or enough food to put on the table?"

Before New Radicals can select a new role for ourselves, we must first discover what calls out to us. What pressing needs do we want to help meet? We're looking for answers to the next question, "What does the world need?"

Chapter 5

What Does the World Need?

More than 450 slave workers—some as young as 14—have been rescued from Chinese brick factories. Working 16 to 20 hours a day, they had been fed just enough to stay alive, and beaten by their captors. At least 13 people died before the government stepped in, in one of the biggest police investigations into forced labor camps in the country.

—*The Guardian Weekly*, June 2007

The answer to the question posed by this chapter, "What does the world need?" is that the human beings and our environment need so much. As any glance at the headlines shows, we are a people and a planet in distress. In fact, the problem that has served as our collective wake-up call—global warming—has intensified since I began to write. An island the size of England breaking free of Canada's largest Arctic ice shelf is the latest disturbing example.

New Radicals-in-the-making have a powerful urge to help. But, sometimes, they are at a loss for where to begin. Even here, at this stage in the journey, having come so far, with so much hope, they talk about being pulled into a vortex of despair. The problems are so big and people so corrupt that it's all just a terrible mess. They sometimes ask themselves: "What can *I* possibly do?" I gently remind them that it's natural to feel this way in the face of so much need. And I point out that there are an infinite number of ways to bring relief, hope, and joy to our fellow human beings, and healing to our planet. We take a deep breath together and talk about how even the smallest gesture can have an immediate and tangible effect.

But if a particular issue or need doesn't immediately present itself—say, "I'm going to work with street children in Rio de Janeiro"—how do you decide? You may be taken aback to discover that the answer to this question begins with us. At this suggestion, traditionalists shift uncomfortably; we have this notion that service is supposed to be self*less.* And even if the motivation that got us onto this path was self*ish,* surely it's time to think of others?

Yes and no. Clearly, it's about making a difference in the world, but we need to find something that calls out to us—that captures our hearts and fires our imagination. Why? Because our enthusiasm will inspire us to take on the challenge and give us the strength to carry on in the face of inevitable difficulties. As Rocco Rossi put it when talking about choosing which nonprofit organization to work for: "I also realized that there would have to be a personal link . . . If I didn't have a commitment to the cause, it would be too easy to bail—to pull the rip cord—when things got tough." Or, consider Elizabeth and Stephen Alderman, whom you read about in Chapter 2. Yes, their work with trauma survivors meets an enormous need, but it also has deep personal meaning. The fact that it's a perfect fit helps them to keep going—and it has contributed to their growing success. Now that New Radicals have a better sense of their deeper selves, they are in a much better position to find something that gives them this kind of connection.

The rewards of good works are immediate; we see that we are making a difference in people's lives. But did you know that research shows that service gives more than it takes? One of my clients sat upright when we were talking about this.

"I totally get that. In business, treating clients well increases the likelihood they'll be back."

"Exactly!" I replied. "Doing good brings endless benefits to the giver. For instance, when we help others, we find meaning in what we do. Our self-esteem grows. We live longer, stay healthier, and experience less stress. In one study of war veterans, those with altruistic tendencies were less likely to develop posttraumatic stress disorder."

"Someone will have to study the New Radicals," he suggested with a grin, and we both laughed.

And then we began to talk in practical terms about how to discover the very thing that spoke to him, and to imagine how he might make a difference. It's not rocket science, I said kindly to his hopeful face, it's good, old-fashioned networking and research.

Where my clients start depends on who they are. If they are outgoing and feel comfortable approaching people directly, I suggest that they pick up the phone—as Rocco Rossi and Victoria Hale did—and take someone interesting to lunch. Most people will readily share what they know and help us in our quest (in fact, as this movement grows, I predict there will be more and more of this mentoring). "Even if not," I say, "you will have gained valuable information, and the encounter will encourage you to keep going." I recommend getting out there in general—widening one's circle of contacts and deepening one's understanding of the world's challenges—by attending workshops, lectures, and conferences. I also urge everyone to read, read, read: "Read mainstream media, special interest publications, and online sources. Read what you usually do—but with a fresh eye. And peruse publications you would normally never pick up." If you subscribe to *The Economist*, sign up for a year of *GOOD*, a magazine which describes itself as a platform for the ideas, people, and organizations that are driving change in the world. If you devour *Vogue* each month, try *Ode* for a change. This magazine is positioned as being "for intelligent optimists" and is full of stories about people who are making a difference.

And, as we've been talking about throughout the entire process, I suggest that budding New Radicals pay attention: "Notice what catches your eye, write it down, and reflect on it." Finally, I encourage them to keep their search as wide as possible initially,

Ex.

Ex.

Good Magazine

and to let it narrow naturally over time, as their interests become clearer—as they begin to see how, exactly, they might help.

As a budding New Radical, you'll be delighted, I think, with the range of options that arise for you: it may be a hot spot on the global stage, or something down the street; an organization that is international, or a good idea that calls out to be developed further to help even more people. In general, though, the search for New Radical answers can be grouped into three categories: start with a deep passion, start close to home, or start with what cries out for help.

START WITH A DEEP PASSION

Many New Radicals follow their hearts. An idea or issue captivates them, and this becomes their starting point. Vinod Khosla, for instance, wants to save the world from oil. Khosla is enthusiastic about a particular kind of ethanol made from agricultural waste. *The Economist* said that he's making the rounds with a "mind-numbing" PowerPoint presentation "unveiled with the affection that some men reserve for pictures of their grandchildren." People are listening, because he's got a great track record: Khosla helped found Sun Microsystems, and then he made a second fortune as a partner in a venture-capital firm that was an early investor in AOL, Amazon, Compaq, and Google. This takes him out of the realm of mere mortals, I realize, but he's a great example for New Radicals because, as he invests his Internet fortune in his new company, Khosla Ventures, he's made it abundantly clear that he does not intend to lose money. He's part of a growing field of green venture capitalists who believe that clean energy can satisfy both their idealism and their bottom line.

Others spring into action when their bliss isn't shared by others. Such is the case with Martin LeBlanc. Manager of volunteer-led programs at the Sierra Club, Martin told me that interest in the great outdoors is dropping among young Americans. For example, between 1995 and 2005, overnight stays at parks such as Yellowstone and Yosemite fell by 20 percent, and camping and backpacking trips by 24 percent. This doesn't bode well for the future of organizations such as the Sierra Club, not to mention our planet. "If this young generation hasn't fallen in love with the natural world in all its splendor, how can we expect them to hold conservationist views?" So he and his team developed a series of volunteer-led programs designed to help bring inner-city children into contact with nature. "At this age, we don't need to give them propaganda about offshore drilling. We just need to get them outside."

In contrast, New Radical Innovator Dr. Martin Seligman's passion was enough to shift an entire field. Positive psychology turned his discipline upside down, and his pioneering thinking has influenced more than his colleagues and their patients: as we learned in Chapter 4, "positive" is part of the New Radical credo.

And sometimes our passion catches us unaware. That certainly was true for Wendy Kopp. Wendy, age 39, grew up in what she describes as a "reasonably privileged" community and went to a "very good" public school. While studying at Princeton, she discovered that others had had very different precollege opportunities and that, despite being some of the most brilliant and driven people she knew, these individuals struggled to meet the academic standards. "I realized that, in our country, which aspires so admirably to be a land of opportunity, where you're born can determine your outcome."

Wendy, of course, is not the first person to notice this. What makes her a New Radical is that she did something to address this inequity. She started Teach for America, a national agency that supplies teachers to communities in need (the Peace Corps is a good parallel). "My idea was to get the best and brightest college students to sign up to teach in this country's rural and inner-city schools."

It was a fantastic idea but, as you can imagine, it was not easy to get off the ground. As she made the rounds, talking to school boards and investors, there was nearly universal enthusiasm, but an equal measure of doubt. "Everywhere I went, people thought it was a great idea, but that 'college students won't ever do that.' We were the 'Me Generation,' and all we supposedly wanted to do was work on Wall Street and make a lot of money." Wendy persevered and managed to raise seed money and gifts in kind from early believers such as Mobil, Morgan Stanley, Merck, and Apple. That was enough to get Teach for America off the ground and launch its first grassroots recruitment campaign—the organization was looking for achievement-oriented, committed graduating seniors. "Within four months, 2,500 students had applied."

Listening to Wendy, I knew she was the classic New Radical: idealistic, for sure, but savvy enough to make things happen. I said that this huge enrollment must have felt like an incredible endorsement of her vision, and heard her voice catch just a little. "Standing up in front of five hundred young, hopeful people with their bright faces, as they set out on their first year, knowing the blood, sweat, and tears that had come together to make that moment possible, and that a huge, steep learning curve lay ahead for all of us; well, it's a moment I'll never forget."

And here's the latest vote of confidence. Teach for America is now one of the largest recruiters of college students in the country—bigger than Microsoft, Procter & Gamble, and General Electric. In fact, the organization is doing so well that some big companies are partnering with it as a way to enhance their own reputations on campus. "The idea is that students will work with us for two years and then move on to a job with a major corporation."

Other New Radicals had talked about the importance the right people can make to an organization, and Wendy reinforces this point: "We were very careful in drafting our mission statement—'to enlist our country's most promising future leaders in the effort to eliminate education inequality'—because we knew that, in education, like in any organization, people are everything." Members believed that if they could recruit tomorrow's leaders, it would be a life-changing experience for the students and a path-changing one for the teachers. Despite tempting deals with prestigious firms, many alumni really *do* change paths as a result of this experience—and continue along New Radical lines. Sixty percent of approximately 12,000 alumni are now working full time in education. And if they do go into other sectors, they tend to do things that are related: advising mayors and governors, leading pro bono initiatives at law firms, or marshalling the resources of medical schools to improve math and science education in local public schools. "They're in significant leadership roles already, despite being in their twenties and thirties."

Teach for America is such a great idea, and I was so moved when speaking with Wendy that I confessed to wishing I were younger so that I could sign up. She responded with all the enthusiasm of a seasoned recruiter, telling me that they recently launched a parallel organization called the New Teacher Project to help school districts set up programs to recruit talented people—young professionals, midcareer professionals, and retired professionals—to teach in underserved areas. "This is for people who are further along in their careers, Julia, and who have roots in a particular community. In New York City alone, 20,000 people applied to be teaching fellows last year. And about 6,000 are in the system now."

START CLOSE TO HOME

Africa is the new Europe. While baby boomers backpacked across a small subcontinent steeped in history, our children are finding their way around a huge landmass with deep need. I asked Stephen Lewis, former U.N. Special Envoy for HIV/AIDS in Africa, for his thoughts on why these 54 countries have captured the imagination of a generation. "There is this sense that Africa is the beleaguered continent—the most impoverished, disease-ridden, and conflict-torn place on Earth. Where people are struggling terribly and very often losing the battle. It calls out to us."

All true. Yet there is also enormous need in our own backyards, and though the media spotlight is often pointed in other directions, New Radicals are increasingly aware of the work that needs doing here at home. The Bill and Melinda Gates Foundation—best known for its massive campaigns in Africa—started out this way. They helped U.S. schools and libraries to develop computer resources. And you'll recall Kye Marshall asking herself whether it made sense to go to a developing country to help: "What good would it do to go to Botswana to dig wells? I'm a trained musician! Wasn't there some way I could use my skills to help?"

At age 50, Aditya Jha is a perfect example of this principle in action. By chance, he attended a dinner where the grand chief of the Nishnawbe Aski Nation, Stan Beardy, was speaking. "My people are suffering," Beardy told the black-tie crowd. Aditya was shocked by this statement and the reality it conveyed. "As an immigrant to Canada, I wondered how is it that these people aren't sharing in the prosperity that I've enjoyed since coming to this country?" He responded by establishing a foundation that underwrites a series of programs designed to help these communities learn the business skills he believes will lift them out of poverty, including one that pairs aboriginal youth with corporate executives—a kind of job shadowing. Even better, his New Radical role is part of a growing trend in the aboriginal community. Native leaders are embracing entrepreneurship and microlending as a way to help their communities. "If they develop their own revenue, they can address complex social problems without relying on government help."

One of my favorite examples of this kind of reverse NIMBY-ism—yes, in my backyard, or YIMBY—is National Basketball Association player Stephon Marbury, age 30. Stephon was concerned that kids feel pressured to buy expensive clothing, including pricey basketball shoes—something that, growing up poor in Brooklyn, he had experienced firsthand. So, he decided to use his fame to make a low-priced shoe popular. His New York Knicks' salary may be $17 million, but he wears $15 shoes when he's on the court.

Don Stannard-Friel, age 63, didn't have to go far afield to create a New Radical role for himself. Don is a professor of sociology and anthropology at Notre Dame de Namur University in Belmont, a leafy suburb of San Francisco. Today, many of his classes are conducted in the inner city—the infamous Tenderloin district.

After we were introduced, I realized that Don would be the only "old radical" in my book: his life parallels the major events of a generation. A kid from New Jersey, he moved to San Francisco "at the end of the beatnik period and the beginning of the free speech era." In 1966, he got married, became a father, and moved to Haight-Ashbury. He was studying at San Francisco State College when "all hell broke loose." As his political consciousness was awakening—and while going to antiwar demonstrations with his baby on his back—he began to study sociology. "My professors were using the cultural revolution taking place all around us as their material, and they were doing ethnographic studies—going into the field with us." While working toward his Ph.D., Don worked in a psychiatric hospital, and he became part of the mental patients civil rights movement. Over the next decade, he completed his degrees, got divorced, and remarried. "We had a hippie wedding in Golden Gate Park and lived communally for a number of years. They were wonderful times."

After several decades of teaching, Don was feeling the need to clear his mind and refresh his spirit. He took a break and headed to the Tenderloin district where he'd lived as a poor student. He wanted to really get to know the community and write about his experience. When he was ready to return to teaching, he realized that this time it would be different. It would call on every part of him—the young activist, the curious student, the experienced professor, and the man who knew and loved this difficult part of a world-famous city. Don designed a series of courses that would take his students into the community, interacting with local people so that they could learn from them and help them at the same time. It's the ideal intersection of what he had to offer and what his young charges wanted. "It's perfect for this new generation. They're not interested in political activism like we were. These kids were raised on community service—it was part of their curriculum from when they were quite small. They want to *do* things, to make a difference. It's quite a shift from my generation."

His students love what's affectionately known as "Tenderloin U." and all that it has to offer, such as a street retreat, where they spend up to a week with a homeless person. Even kids who don't show much enthusiasm for traditional studies show up for Don's classes. "It's hard for suburban students to get into San Francisco and find where we're working each day. But they do it without fail." As you might expect, the idea initially wasn't popular in all quarters; there was considerable resistance from Mom and Dad. "I had parents calling me and saying, 'I'm spending $35,000 to send my kid to university, and you're taking her to the Tenderloin?'" But now that it's working so well and students are so enthusiastic, there's widespread support.

Don totally understands this apprehension. The Tenderloin can seem scary if you aren't able to decode what's going on—such as drug deals taking place on street corners in broad daylight, which students spot right away. "It gives us a chance to talk about containment zones: the idea that if you don't contain crimes, they just move to another block." The bottom line, he says, is that this may be an unusual part of the city, but it's also a safe one. One of the central questions posed by Don's course is, "Why do so many children love living here?" The answer is that kids sense that they are watched over, and feel safe. The neighborhood is home to lots of immigrant families, many of whom live in small, cramped spaces. As a result, everyone ends up outside. Hang out long enough, and you figure out that the raised voices aren't arguments but simply people calling to one another up, down, and across the streets, as villagers in the old country might have done.

Like other New Radicals, Don discovered that relationships paved the way for his new work, giving him street credibility. He lived here as a young man, some 40 years ago and, more recently, spent time getting to know people in the area. "Someone will look at me and say, 'Who's this white guy with his white beard?' and I'll mention someone I think they might know. Either they relax immediately, or they check me out and figure out that we're here to help."

Don has also developed a good working relationship with the local police, something this former hippie never imagined himself doing. For instance, the police are part of the Tenderloin Halloween party: they bring food for 400 or so children each year. "When I was young, it was all about 'we've got to change the world through revolution!'" Today, he's more open to other people's points of view, and he talks to his students about what he now believes is true: that it's all about making a difference in a single person's life. "I tell them, when you change a person's life, they change others, and the people they touch do the same. It becomes a geometric progression. It doesn't take long before you're changing thousands of lives, all because of that one person."

START WITH WHAT CRIES OUT FOR HELP

Sometimes the call is so clear and so unequivocal that we feel compelled to respond. New Radical pioneer Muhammad Yunus is certainly in this camp. As a professor of economics in Bangladesh, he was distressed to learn that women from a nearby village were being charged extortionate rates of interest, thereby ensuring that they would have to endure a lifetime of penury. He lent them money, and this gesture grew into the now widespread practice of microlending, his world-famous Grameen Bank, and, ultimately, to his being awarded the Nobel Peace Prize for this work. (The Grameen Bank lends to poor people with little or no credit history. Low-cost loans mean that the poorest of the poor can begin to build futures for themselves. This practice has been so successful in Bangladesh that Muhammad predicts that the country will have eliminated extreme poverty within 10 years.)

Or consider Mary Gordon. After more than 30 years in education, Mary believes that empathy—the ability to identify with another person's feelings—is the single most important skill we can teach children. It helps them immediately and sets them up for life. "As empathy rises," Mary said simply, "aggression falls."

Mary founded Roots of Empathy, a program whereby certified instructors visit primary schools to help students learn the valuable skill of empathy. Every three weeks, the instructor and a parent and infant from the neighborhood sit on a blanket surrounded by students. The children observe the baby, ask questions, and talk about how she is developing. "They learn to follow the baby's lead and read her cues." Because changes in an infant are dramatic and visible, children soon figure out what a baby is telling them. In doing so, they become more attuned to their own feelings and to those of others. In one classroom, for example, a particularly aggressive and belligerent child was a concern. The parent, teacher, and instructor conferred and decided to position him directly beside the baby. "Imagine his reaction when the baby smiled at him!" During the second visit, this little boy took off his ever-present hat whenever he was near the child. "On the third visit, he brought a feather to tickle her foot. He had clearly been changed." What's more, from that point on, the teacher and other students saw him from a new and kinder point of view, and he was incorporated into the social life of his class.

Mary Gordon, you could say, is saving the world classroom by classroom. Dr. Victoria Hale, on the other hand, is taking it one disease at a time—and in the most unusual way.

When Victoria and I find time to talk, one of the first things we touch on is how she began to reinvent her career. Like so many New Radicals, it didn't come to her in a "voilà!" moment one morning but emerged gradually. "It was more like sand in the oyster. You know, irritation . . . *Frustration* is a better word." The source of her frustration? She knew that some people in the world had lots of medicines available to them, and others were actually going to have fewer and fewer over time. The reason is economic. In the West we have a pharmaceutical industry working on our behalf, to make new medications for us, but billions of people in the world don't enjoy this privilege. This situation is particularly true in regard to infectious diseases, where resistance means there always has to be something fresh coming along to combat them. "So, throughout my first career, I was worrying away at this bit of sand." Victoria had been a scientist in the pharmaceutical industry, as well as an official at the U.S. Food and Drug Administration (FDA). At the FDA, she worked with hundreds of companies on thousands of different drug development programs. And that's where she first saw firms making the decision to leave certain disease areas. "They would come to the business conclusion that other diseases offered better opportunities." Drugs in development were stopped because they weren't going to make the company grow.

This realization was underscored when she went to work for a biotechnology company. "We were developing dazzling medicines, focusing narrowly on specific diseases. The end result was success, but it also meant that fewer and fewer people had access." Cancer is a case in point. A company can go after one type of breast cancer, focus all of its efforts there, and cure people with that kind of cancer. But what about other types of breast cancer, or cancer in general? And what about the large numbers of deaths due to pathogens and other causes we don't have in our world? "Ninety percent of the world's diseases are in developing countries, but just 3 percent of research and development is directed at them."

When she was in her late thirties, Victoria had reached a point in her career that is familiar to New Radicals. She had a sense of mastery, having achieved many of her goals. Yet, at the same time, she was losing enthusiasm for what she was doing. "The fact that I could see the rest of my life laid out before me was unsettling." She also longed to do something bigger, something more stimulating, something that would really make a difference. She knew that she needed to move from frustration to clarity, so she quit her job. From what I've heard of Victoria, work has always been central to her life, so this must have been a tough call. She readily acknowledged that she's a workaholic. "I hadn't taken time off since graduate school. But I knew I needed time to think more about what I could do that was engaging and challenging for me, but would also have an impact on the world." She had planned to take three months off, and later extended it to six months. All the while she was thinking about two things of which she was certain: first, she was a good medicine maker and wanted to continue in that field; second, she wanted to do it for larger numbers of people.

Victoria began her research in the Bay Area, which is full of people who have started biotech companies. As she made the rounds, an idea began to grow. She saw that the for-profit model would take her down the same path she had been on and would lead to the obstacles she'd already encountered. "I realized I would be starting the world's first nonprofit pharmaceutical company." When she started to talk about that, people told her she was crazy. "A few said I would ruin my reputation. And one CEO, I won't name names, actually patted me on the head!" But when she started talking about it as an experiment—when she would say "you're a scientist, and this is an experiment"—she got a few more nods. For a year and a half, she traveled the world talking to people in the global health field, asking them what work on promising drugs had come very close to success but then been stopped—she was looking for near-term successes that had been set aside. And then, in 2000, she founded the Institute for OneWorld Health, with a mandate to develop safe, effective, and affordable medicines for infectious diseases in the third world.

Leishmaniasis was OneWorld Health's first choice—a parasitic infection transmitted by the bite of a sand fly, and common in Bangladesh, Brazil, India, Nepal, and Sudan. Victoria approached the World Health Organization to ask if her company could take over trials of an injectable form of paromomycin. "And they said yes!" For a brand-new company, and a nonprofit to boot, this was a significant accomplishment. And another important ally would soon signal its support for what she was doing: the Bill and Melinda Gates Foundation contributed the funds needed to get the project off the ground. "OneWorld Health also partnered with four health-care centers in India to test the drug against an established but much more expensive treatment—about $130 compared to $10." The trials were an unconditional success. The new drug quickly got regulatory approval in India, was submitted to the FDA in 2007, and was written up in the June 21, 2007, issue of *The New England Journal of Medicine.*

While this early success was welcome, it also meant they were on the right track. They knew for certain that their innovative model worked: assemble an experienced and dedicated team; identify the most promising drug and vaccine candidates and develop them into medicines; then partner with companies, nonprofit hospitals, and organizations in the developing world to conduct research, manufacture, and distribute.

Victoria is too modest to mention that she won a MacArthur Foundation "Genius" Award for her work with OneWorld Health, which sounds to me like she's entered the greatest contribution territory that New Radicals believe possible. But she's happy to talk about what's next on the agenda for her organization: diarrhea. Many people think it's a disease, but it's really a symptom of an illness caused by bacteria, a virus, or a parasite. If not properly treated, it can lead to life-threatening fluid loss, which can kill a young child in just a few hours. "In the developing world, 2 million babies—children under five—die every year from diarrhea, Julia. That's more than from tuberculosis, AIDS, and malaria combined." Standard treatment is oral rehydration, and OneWorld Health is investigating a companion treatment, such as a low-cost medicine to build up a victim's defenses and allow time for the infection to clear. A $46 million grant from the Gates Foundation will finance preclinical studies, which include partners in Belgium, the United Kingdom, and Bangladesh. After that, drug manufacturers may be brought in to take the product to market.

And then Victoria said something that made me want to high-five every emerging New Radical Innovator around the world—people who want to continue in their current roles while helping to change their organizations from within: "The world's top pharmaceutical and biotechnology companies have come calling: they want to partner with us, saying they are eager to play a role in eliminating these neglected diseases, too. That it would make their staff proud to be doing this work."

ASK NOT WHAT THE WORLD CAN DO FOR YOU

I've heard people refer to New Radicals as "do-gooders." To me, this is pejorative and reminds me of the executive who patted Victoria Hale on the head. It also, of course, misses the point. New Radicals are smart, sophisticated, successful people who are doing extraordinary things in a world that sorely needs our help.

While the humanitarian and environmental reasons to act are compelling, the economic and political arguments are alarming. In presenting these reasons here, I realize that I am preaching to the choir. But I believe that even you and I need to be reminded of the facts from time to time—it's just too easy to put them out of our minds. As Ron Dembo said while we were sitting in a park talking about his new environmental company, Zerofootprint: "It's hard to believe that anything's wrong, isn't it? It's a beautiful day. We've eaten well. Life is good. What crisis?" If you're reading this book while lying in bed or sitting in a comfortable chair, you'll be able to relate to how Ron and I felt that afternoon. It's hard to really *know* that someone didn't eat today, that somebody died unnecessarily, or that the world's oceans may soon be beyond repair.

The case for action keeps getting louder.

For instance, in 2006, the TD Bank Financial Group released a report detailing the reasons to combat AIDS in developing countries. Don Drummond, the bank's chief economist and author of the report, said that countries in sub-Saharan Africa have HIV infection rates of up to 25 percent and that, while previous research showed that each country's gross national product (GNP) would be slowed by about half a percent, he believes this "grossly underestimates" the problem. He pointed out that affected countries are losing massive numbers of people who should be entering their prime working years, and their children—now AIDS orphans—are less likely to get an education. "Some of these countries are looking at complete devastation if we don't do something now. And if we don't do something now, it will end up costing more in every way later on."

A report by the British economist Sir Nicholas Stern, published in late 2006, and covered extensively by the media, suggests that global warming could shrink the global economy by 20 percent, but that taking action now would cost just 1 percent of global gross domestic product (GDP).

In 2007, climate change was also recognized by the U.N. Security Council—not just narrow, national security, but collective security in our increasingly interdependent world. Peering into the future, the Council made it clear that this will not be the first time that people have fought over land, water, and resources, but this time it will be on a scale that dwarfs conflicts of the past.

In April of the same year, the Military Advisory Board, composed of retired American admirals and generals—about as far from tree huggers as one can imagine—released a report that states unequivocally that climate change poses a threat to national security.

If the opportunities to help are endless, the reasons to do so are becoming increasingly clear.

YOUR JOURNEY CONTINUES

By now, the New Radicals in my consulting room feel more like horses chafing at the bit. With a clear overview of their abilities, insight into what's important to them, and a solid grasp of the issues, it's time to run with it. They are ready to answer the central question of this journey: "What is your new role?"

Chapter 6

What Is Your New Role?

One of the world's last hunter-gatherer tribes is facing a new threat. The Hadzabe's demise is being hastened by a United Arab Emirates royal family. A spokesman says they intend to use this ancient tribe's hunting grounds near the Serengeti as a personal safari playground. It was selected after a helicopter tour of the area.

—*The Guardian Weekly*, June 2007

Picture a bustling marketplace, overflowing with colorful and tantalizing displays. This is where New Radicals find themselves: an array of options is before them, and they are about to select something to nourish the second half of their working lives. They typically report a strong emotional response at this milestone—*verklempt* is how one client put it with a crooked grin, as she fanned away the tears. Suddenly, it's clear that what they have been longing for is actually going to come true.

Many pause for a moment to look over their shoulders. So often, our first careers were what others wanted us to do. Dr. Mark Grabowsky went off to the naval academy because that's what the Grabowsky men did. Others, such as Melissa Dyrdahl, described it as getting on a track that was easy: "I got started on this wonderful path, and opportunities kept coming my way. But eventually it becomes the path of least resistance." Would it comfort you to know that you're not alone? Even some of the world's most successful people were originally encouraged to do something totally different. Joseph Campbell was strongly urged to take over the family business. George Frideric Handel was told that he should become a lawyer. And Isaac Newton's family wanted him to farm.

This is not to say that our first careers were not important. *Au contraire*. In fact, as I was researching this book, the phrase "from success to significance" kept popping up. To me, that doesn't quite capture it. In fact, many New Radicals bristled at the suggestion that their first occupation was anything less than important. Who could say that Mark Brayne, Dr. Victoria Hale, Kye Marshall, and Kevin Salwen were doing something insignificant in their early years? But, this time, we are choosing for ourselves.

We're quite specific about what we want from this role—that our deepest desires and hard-won adult capabilities are put to work in service of the greater good.

You may have noticed that I describe what New Radicals do as a "role." I chose the word carefully. Clearly, our work is so much more than a job, but "role" also captures the idea that we are each playing a part in the unfolding of this movement—one part in a play that is much larger than us.

Now, what about that role? Just as we discovered parts of ourselves that we'd forgotten, here, we begin to see that the world is full of possibilities. While the opportunities are endless, those chosen by New Radicals fall into one of three categories: Activists, Entrepreneurs, and Innovators. As explained in Chapter 1, Activists are those who actively serve the less fortunate. For instance, they may move from the corporate to nonprofit sector, or carve significant time out of their busy schedules to take on a second, helping role. In contrast, Entrepreneurs start new enterprises where making a difference is an integral part of their work. And then there are the Innovators, people who remain in their current role and influence their organization or field from within. New Radical roles fall somewhere along the continuum from mild to wild. We may decide to sell everything on eBay and move to a village in Rwanda like Nicole Pageau, modify our business as Jamie Kennedy has done, or build a New Radical career from day one like Wendy Kopp. My clients say that this is what is so great about this movement. Not only can they find a role that is aligned with who they are, what they have to offer, and how they want to help, but also it can be as out there or as conservative as they want it to be.

Sometimes our new role is offered to us. For example, Ayisi Makatiani was born in Kenya, educated in America's best schools, and returned home to launch Africa's first Internet service provider. He was raising funds to start a private equity firm when he caught the eye of one of his potential investors—the International Finance Corporation, the World Bank's private-sector arm. They persuaded him to run the African Management Services Company, charged with helping African firms become competitive. When asked if he ever imagined becoming a New Radical, his response is a bark of laughter: "Suddenly I'm a man with a mission. All my friends thought I'd gone mad!" Another particularly delightful example popped up as I reread Martin Seligman's *Authentic Happiness.* I discovered that not only is Seligman a New Radical, but so are many members of his team. For instance, Seligman writes that he contacted Dr. Christopher Peterson, one of the world's leading authorities on hope and optimism and director of the clinical psychology program at the University of Michigan, to ask him to help develop the strengths classification system. "As I waited for his polite refusal, I was stunned when Chris said, 'What a strange coincidence. Yesterday was my fiftieth birthday, and I was just sitting here—in my first midlife crisis—wondering what I was going to do with the rest of my life . . . So, I accept.'"

Most often, however, New Radicals either find an existing position or create one for themselves. "Your task now," I say to my clients, "is to get specific." As Rocco Rossi realized, when you are still uncertain, everyone applauds your desire to save the world, but no one knows what to do with you.

Some of us just *know* what we want to do, which is something my clients not-so-secretly wish will happen to them—

having a ready answer to this chapter's question is the New Radical equivalent of winning the lottery. "So, you're not expecting an epiphany?" I said to one client, echoing what she'd just shared. "Well, I'm not ruling one out, either!" she replied quickly, her words crashing into mine. For most of us, though, it takes lots of thought, the identification of a range of options, and weighing the pros and cons of each.

How do New Radicals create this clarity for themselves? The decision typically comes one of three ways: as a natural next step, through a flash of inspiration, or as a breakthrough.

TAKE THE NATURAL NEXT STEP

Once they had done their homework, certain New Radicals found that their new role came quickly into focus. They saw it as an obvious choice and as being within reach.

What's the most natural evolution for New Radicals? To become Activists—that is, to do similar work in a different sector, most often the nonprofit world. Interestingly, this migration couldn't come at a better time. The magnitude of the talent shortage faced by mission-driven organizations was underlined in a report published in 2006 by the Bridgespan Group, "The Nonprofit Sector's Leadership Deficit" [Executive Summary, page 2]: "Over the next decade, these organizations will need to attract and develop some 640,000 new senior managers—the equivalent of 2.4 times the number currently employed." And that's just in the United States. My own research confirms this projection. Plus, as I wrote this section, the William J. Clinton and Skoll foundations were looking for people, the Bill and Melinda Gates Foundation reported that it expected to double its staff in the next few years, and a number of the New Radicals organizations you have read about told me they were hiring.

Like millions of other boomers (as much as one-third of this generation, and climbing), New Radicals are also saying that they want to become Entrepreneurs. They're tired of working for others, and they want to set up shop on their own. As Melissa Dyrdahl put it: "I had a really strong entrepreneurial spirit that was dying to get out." Dr. Victoria Hale is a prime example of this trend in action. First, she realized that she would have to start a company if she were going to achieve her goal of making medicines for the world's poor. And, soon after, it dawned on her that the world's first nonprofit pharmaceutical company was the natural next step. "The for-profit model would just take me down the same path and lead to the same obstacles I'd encountered."

Other budding New Radicals are established entrepreneurs who change their practices to bring them in line with their deepest beliefs, while meeting the needs of this emerging movement. Sean Stannard-Stockton is a case in point. We first heard about him through his dad, Don Stannard-Friel. When Sean and I connected, we talked about how his field—financial planning—is evolving. A second wave of philanthropy is being driven by the baby boom generation, some of whom have done well (amassing great wealth, either themselves or through inheritance) and now want to do good. So, Sean has shifted his practice to serve the needs of this growing sector. "For instance, my clients might want to start a private foundation or a charitable trust. What's the best way to achieve their goals?" There's a growing need for knowledgeable professionals, and Sean is one of just three people in the United States who holds both Chartered Financial Planner and Chartered Advisor in Philanthropy designations.

There are thousands of these stories, many more than I can share, but two arrived in my e-mail inbox as I was writing, which show how New Radicals in different parts of the world are coming to similar conclusions about what to do next. In California, Linda and Trent McNair have started a company—Surf City Growers—that produces organic bedding plants and sells them online. What motivated them was what usually motivated others: they had had enough of corporate life, a feeling that intensified as they started their family. They wanted to combine their passion for gardening with a desire to save the planet. Says Linda: "When a former egg ranch came on the market, we jumped at the chance to turn it into an organic nursery."

Half a world away, in Abu Dhabi, Khalid Al-Shamsi is changing the emirate's perspective on the environment and improving the health of its citizens. Chairman of Abu Dhabi Organics Group, he is growing fruit and vegetables in the red-hued sands of the region. "We want to be the first locally produced, organic produce in the market." What can grow in sand and heat? Khalid mentioned sweet potatoes, mangoes, asparagus, and lemongrass as being among the edibles that could be grown.

My own story is another example. Shifting to midlife coaching was a natural next step for me. After all, I had been listening carefully to my clients—CEOs, cabinet ministers, and celebrities—for years as they told me their stories and shared their goals. Writing speeches for them, I realized, was more than putting their vision into words. I was creating a narrative that would help shape their careers and their organizations, while influencing their audiences. Surely I could use the same skills to help people imagine their futures.

All of this was on my mind when I went to see Don Raymond, who had also taken a step that could be described as a natural evolution for a New Radical. Don, age 46, left a lucrative job on Wall Street to become senior vice president and head of public market investments for the Canada Pension Plan Investment Board (CPPIB). As we sat in his office overlooking Lake Ontario, I asked him why he made the move and realized that he had a classic category one wake-up call. He was looking for a challenge and a way to give back. "It was born partly out of intellectual curiosity—in this work, there are a lot of challenges, we're doing innovative things and, for most of it, there is no book you can take off the shelf. And there was also a service component—I'd describe it instead as a sense of duty."

Don's challenge was to help this fledgling fund—the investment arm of the Canada Pension Plan—find its wings. The CPPIB manages a fund that will help sustain the pensions of 16 million Canadians. In 2000, it had assets of CDN$44 billion. By June 2006, the fund had more than doubled to $98 billion, and by June 30, 2007, it had reached $120 billion. By 2016, it is expected to be worth $250 billion. Net contributions and returns on the portfolio are behind this extraordinary growth, always undertaken with an eye to maximizing returns without undue risk. "Our objective is to invest in the best interest of contributors and beneficiaries. So everything we do is put in a risk and return context." Today, the fund is diversifying and invests across all asset classes, in many economic sectors, and around the world.

And it is the ownership of publicly traded equities that triggered the need for a policy on how to invest responsibly.

CPPIB is the first pension fund in Canada to have such a policy, called the Policy on Responsible Investing. Don was at the table as the United Nations developed its Principles on Responsible Investing—voluntary guidelines to incorporate environmental, social, and governance (ESG) issues into mainstream investment decision making. And CPPIB's own policy was developed in tandem with this process. CPPIB is also the first pension fund in Canada to have a staff member dedicated to responsible investing, a role that is part of Don's team. "That's a clear signal that we see this as part of the investment side of our business and not simply, for instance, a public relations issue."

To understand responsible investing, one needs to know what came before. Social investing had traditionally relied on what's known as screening—that is, entire industries were considered bad investments based on nonfinancial criteria (for example, the tobacco industry). CPPIB didn't want to abandon progressive investing—"we do believe that there are issues in the environmental, social, and governance realms that are important"—but decided that engagement was a better approach. "It's all about engaging with companies and encouraging them to improve their practices, so that their risk premium shrinks and their share prices rise."

Don offered Xstrata, the Swiss mining company, as an example. When Xstrata went public in 2002, it produced a 400-page prospectus that contained just one line about climate risk. At that time, its business relied on high-sulfur coal, and one of its largest customers was in Japan. One month after the company went public, the Japanese government mused publicly about carbon taxes. In one day, Xstrata's stock dropped 8 percent; within the month, it was 30 percent lower. Don doesn't need to have a personal view on climate change to do his job, but he does need to know whether regulators believe the problem is created by human beings—because if they do impose regulations, that will cost the company and affect the return on capital. "In Xstrata's case, insufficient disclosure on carbon risk affected its investors materially."

CPPIB's policy is clearly part of a growing global trend. Today, hundreds of asset owners, investment managers, and professional service partners from around the world are signatories to the U.N. principles. And CPPIB has also signed up for the Carbon Disclosure Project, the world's largest institutional investor collaboration on the business implications of climate change. It's clear that some of the smartest money managers in the world believe that responsible investing will pay big dividends in the years to come, which seems pretty New Radical to me.

WATCH FOR A FLASH OF INSPIRATION

Remember how Scott Johnson and Nicole Pageau described their wake-up calls—like a bolt out of the blue? A number of New Radicals discovered their roles this way. Consider Dutch actor and TV host Marc Klein Essink. Marc had 20 years of success under his belt when he realized he wanted something more out of life. One day, walking down the street, absentmindedly playing with some coins in his pocket, he wondered how much change he actually had. He took a wild guess and, after counting it, realized he had three times as much. "If I didn't know how much I had, I could easily do without it." In that moment, an idea was born: Marc started a National Day for Change (NDC) in the Netherlands, which encourages people to give their change to charity on that day, with the money going into a pool to support microcredit projects—offering small loans to people at the poverty line—around the world. He now works full time for NDC, in partnership with his business associate Arthur Hoogendijk and retired banker Diederik Laman Trip. In fact, the trio has just taken things to the next level, by launching a program to help schoolchildren understand microcredit. Classes from grades five and six jointly take out a loan, decide how to use it, and learn that anyone really can make something big out of small change.

Brainstorms don't only come when we step away from our normal routine, yet often this is the case. Suzanne Seggerman, age 44, had been a documentary filmmaker for more than 15 years when she took some time off to raise her daughter, Tatiana. As a new mother, she realized that her priorities were changing. "When you have a kid, you start to reconfigure your life. Time becomes incredibly precious. And I didn't want to spend it doing anything that wasn't meaningful."

While she was deciding what she might do next, the editor of one of her films gave her a videogame, *Hidden Agenda*, about Central American politics. She was electrified. "I played for 12 hours straight. It was one of the most exciting media experiences of my life." Apart from being thoroughly entertaining, the game threw open a window to a whole new world for Suzanne. It reminded her of how documentaries had once captured her heart—in the days when they were engaging people with serious content. "All of a sudden, I saw that games were able to educate people even as they were being entertained."

A game developed for the United Nations is a great example. *U.N. Food Force* helps young people learn about feeding people in need: they lead virtual campaigns, manage rations, ride in a helicopter, do food drops, and experience what it's like to be an aid worker. The potential to help young people shift their view of the developing world—and make New Radical career choices—is clear. "'I want to be a humanitarian when I grow up' isn't something you expect to hear teens saying. But, with this game, they just might."

Suzanne began to explore the field and realized that gaming was huge. Worldwide, digital games generate $28 billion annually, and sales in the United States alone regularly outstrip Hollywood box office. About 50 percent of Americans play videogames six or more hours a week, and a game that allows you to control the lives of virtual characters is one of the bestsellers. "*The Sims*—which has sold 6 million copies worldwide—is on par with *Star Wars* for revenue." Clearly, games could be a powerful new way to engage people and help spread the word about the world's most pressing issues.

Suzanne soon found a community within a community: individuals who were beginning to design what are now known as serious games. In 2003, there was just a tiny group of people like her, enough to fit around a table at a digital games conference. "I met with people like Barry Joseph of Global Kids and Benjamin Stokes of NetAid, and we talked about how there were a lot of nonprofits who were interested in such games, or would be if they knew they existed." She cofounded Games for Change, part of the Serious Games Initiative at the Woodrow Wilson International Center for Scholars, to play a role in the development of the industry.

Today, the serious games sector is big enough to have its own conferences. For instance, Games for Change cohosted one with Parsons The New School for Design, where people from the World Bank, UNICEF, and MTV met and mingled. Yet even with these big players onboard, games still have a bad reputation in some circles. "The media tends to fixate on violent and misogynist examples. In fact, 80 percent of the most popular games in the last five years were rated 'E,' for everyone." Rather than trying to control what's out there, Games for Change is focused on creating an environment where more meaningful alternatives will thrive.

Games for Change was clearly the right New Radical role for Suzanne. In fact, the organization is doing so well that it's expanding—and hiring. Suzanne mentions looking for an executive director to free her to do more of what she's good at: sketching out the big picture for people and raising the visibility of what the organization is trying to do. "My job is to make the dialogue about this important and fast-growing sector more nuanced and informed."

ACHIEVE A BREAKTHROUGH

Some New Radicals talked about how, in retrospect, all of the choices they had made in life, everything they had done and learned—sometimes reaching far into the past—had led to what could be described as a breakthrough role. When one of my clients added everything up and found a role for which she is uniquely suited, we laughed about her being "an overnight success." We have already met a number of New Radicals who qualify as breakthroughs, including Don Stannard-Friel, Scott Johnson, David Simms, and Dan O'Brien. Sister Elaine MacInnes is another. MacInnes teaches meditation and yoga to prisoners around the world. She says that it is her dual faith—she is both a Catholic nun and a Zen roshi trained in Japan—that allowed her to create the Free the Spirit program in the first place, and to see it to fruition. "I started Zen to know the Japanese people, but I continued it as a personal discipline in the development of my own spirituality, and finally chose it as my service to others."

There's no doubt that breakthrough roles have led to extraordinary results. Dr. Ed Sutt, age 38, is definitely one of my favorite examples of this principle in action. His story begins with weather—bad weather. In this decade, 14 major storms have caused more than $160 billion in damage across the United States. When considering the costs caused by storms such as Hurricane Katrina—or contemplating the havoc that's to come—most people (and the building codes they create) focus on the structure. But what *really* accounts for so much of the destruction? The failure of fasteners—in a word, nails. They say that necessity is the mother of invention. And now Ed Sutt has reinvented the nail.

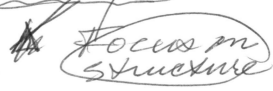

As we began our conversation, Ed made the kind of comment that typifies New Radicals. He worries that people might feel let down because he didn't have a eureka moment: "I have to tell the truth—a lightbulb didn't go off for me." Instead, a long line of events beginning in childhood were responsible for Ed's earning the moniker "Dr. Nail." His dad was an architect-builder, which meant that by the time Ed was seven, he was spending Saturdays on the job site with him. By the time he was 14, Ed was helping his father hammer wooden frames together. As a young man, Ed went off to university to earn an engineering degree, then tried his hand at contracting, found he wasn't much good at it, and went back to earn his master's degree and Ph.D. And this is where the road really rose to meet our hero. To finance school, Ed took a job as a research assistant at Clemson University's Wind Load Test Facility, where they were studying the relationship between wind velocity and the failure of wood-frame structures. Suddenly, all the practical experience about wood-frame houses he'd learned from his dad came in handy. "That part of the puzzle and this one fit perfectly together." Eventually, he was part of a team that flew into the Caribbean islands of St. Thomas and St. Croix, to study the effects of Hurricane Marilyn. While there, Hurricane Opal hit the islands, giving him a front-row seat. At that time he began to see the light. "In house after house, I realized it wasn't the wood that gave way but the nails that were holding it together."

Ed was seized by an idea: he wanted to create a better nail. Doctorate in hand, and with perfect timing, he approached Stanley-Bostitch, the toolmaker giant. The company was just beginning to invest in fastener engineering and gave him a chance to work on something, it's clear in retrospect, he'd spent his entire life preparing for. But the dream and reality were still miles apart. "As I built and tested prototype after prototype, I thought back to watching my dad go through 1,700 different scenarios in his quest to find—based on a number of constraints—the best solution for his clients. I remember thinking as a kid, 'When is this going to end?' Now I see it as a positive influence." A bigger nail head would make a difference, but it couldn't be too big or it wouldn't fit into popular nail guns. The bottom half of the nails would have barbs. Through a lot of testing, Ed discovered that if the barbs are not accurately placed on the sheath, it actually weakens the fastener if you push on it perpendicularly. "You know, like when the big bad wolf tried to blow the house down." Placement and angle of the barbs was really important.

The first nail Ed developed was for pallets. They may not have to withstand the elements, but pallet nails do have to survive the wear and tear of forklifts and the weight of enormous loads. Thanks to a real team effort ("everyone in the company played a role"), the nail did very well in the marketplace and was included in an exhibition at the Museum of Modern Art in New York: "Design Takes on Risk." The success of this nail—and the ensuing attention—spurred the team to action. And, before long, the HurriQuake nail was born. The head is 25 percent bigger than the head on traditional nails, the shank is spiral, and there are angled barbs that help keep it in place, even under the extreme duress of a hurricane or earthquake. Stanley-Bostitch is selling every HurriQuake nail it can produce, is doubling its capacity each month, and intends to go worldwide.

"What's the additional cost of using HurriQuake nails to build a house, Ed?"

"About $15."

And the cost of making the world a little safer? Priceless.

THE NEW RADICALS TO WATCH

Sometimes, New Radicals need more time to choose a new role. The process can take a considerable amount of thought—as well as further exploration of the marketplace—to figure out the next step. I have one client with whom I've worked for a number of years. He has much to offer and many ideas about what he might do, but so far he has resisted making a move. We check in from time to time, and when we last spoke, it occurred to me that he might just become an Innovator.

Naturally, most of the New Radicals I've encountered are—or are in the process of becoming—Activists or Entrepreneurs. It's what these pioneers long to do, and I admire them for being brave groundbreakers. Their stories are the ones that capture the media spotlight and take our breath away. But I have to tell you, Innovators are going to be the ones to watch. Leaving one's organization or field isn't for everyone. There are plenty of examples of New Radicals who stayed where they are and changed the world around them. Jon Kabat-Zinn, for instance, didn't move to India to help feed and clothe the poor. He introduced fresh ideas into the medical profession and helped meditation become an accepted—and immensely useful—part of many people's lives.

Stop and think for a moment. We can't *all* leave our jobs. Everyone can't become ecowarriors, goodwill ambassadors, organic farmers, aid workers, or solar energy salespeople. We can't all get jobs with the World Wildlife Fund, Doctors Without Borders, or Amnesty International. The world needs plumbers and firefighters, sanitation workers and bus drivers, ballerinas and IT specialists. Someone needs to keep the trains running, the banks operating, and the lines of communication open. How will environmentalists get to conferences or aid workers get supplies into the hands of people who need them without infrastructure? Yet each of these people wants to do good, too.

Take heart. Carlos Mesquita is a powerful indicator of things to come. As general manager of international mining company BHP Billiton's new aluminum smelter in southern Mozambique, Carlos knew that malaria was going to be a problem. He saw it spreading across the region and realized that employees would be calling in sick. But even this experienced manager was shocked when a third of his people fell ill, and 13 died. And all of this after the company had taken considerable precautions, such as an on-site medical clinic, treatment of its property with pesticides to kill mosquitoes, and free bed nets for each member of their employees' families. "It was a huge disaster. And it wasn't going to go away. I knew that if we didn't do something, we would lose even more people." And the company stood to lose its $1.3 billion investment. At Carlos's suggestion, the firm joined an innovative public-private partnership. The governments of three countries and a number of corporations worked together to take on malaria, based on a single idea: that the disease could be defeated only with a wide, systematic campaign. The tools were the same (bed nets, pesticides), but the approach was new. And it worked. Today, malaria is in retreat in the region. "Just 1 percent of our workers are away at the moment, and attendance at the local schools is up to normal levels."

Thinking about Carlos, I started to get really excited. What if we all could become New Radicals? Sound impossible? Consider this: organizations are going to have to embrace the emerging New Radicals in their midst or risk losing them. (Just think about the number of times people in this book said, "I quit my job and . . .") It's no secret that millions of baby boomers are itching to reinvent themselves; a New Radical brain drain doesn't have to be the inevitable result. And organizations will have to accommodate them to meet the needs of those I call the Next New Radicals—that is, people in their teens, twenties, and thirties who want to build meaningful careers from the get-go. Already, many of my human resources contacts around the world tell me, companies have discovered that recent graduates are very particular about the packages they'll accept. One need only think of Teach for America to consider how careers are changing. And business schools are another good indicator of things to come. Some of the best and brightest graduates are choosing to work for philanthropies rather than going into the corporate sector. Roger Martin, dean of the Rotman School of Management at the University of Toronto, put it this way: "They're saying, 'I can make a lot of money, or I can have a career with more meaning and a perfectly acceptable lifestyle.'" Boomers may have thought they'd make their millions and then give back, but this cohort wants to do rewarding work now. As one young client put it: "If I'm going to be pulling long hours, I'd like it to be in service of someone in need."

Imagine what it would be like if employees of the world's largest organizations—public or private—knew that they could become Innovators, make decisions based on the New Radical credo, or help drive their organizations to world-saving heights. For those lucky people, "good" wouldn't be what they did after hours but something integrated into what they do each day. Where would you rather work?

DOING WELL, DOING GOOD

If we, as individuals, can discover our New Radical roles, might the world's richest families do so, too? That's the delightful suggestion of author Iris Nowell. In an article in the *Toronto Star*, she wrote that, since Bill Gates and Warren Buffett have already taken on global health, it's time for other wealthy families to step up to the plate. For instance, what if the Waltons—of Wal-Mart, and worth some $60 billion—were to "pass the hat around at a family gathering to tackle environmental problems"? The mind wanders. Who are the world's richest families, and what might they take on? Peace? Poverty? Or what about terrorism? In fact, the Saudis are addressing that issue with a distinctly New Radical approach. They are putting new prisoners through an intensive program aimed at rehabilitating them. The offenders meet in groups with respected clerics—as each inmate raises his rationale for terrorism, the clerics use Islam to refute it. And while we're dreaming, what if, instead of printing lists of the world's richest, the financial press instead publishes information about who's giving away the most this year?

NEW RADICALS ARE ROLLING STONES

Whatever role we choose, it will evolve over time. We have decades ahead of us, and we'll change, as will the world around us. We are still in the early days of this movement, but examples are already emerging that illustrate that the roles we choose today will change. Look at Bill Gates. When he and Melinda first started their foundation, Bill committed 15 hours of his very busy month to this work. In 2006, when he announced that he would be stepping down from his duties at Microsoft the following year to focus on their foundation, financial journalists widely played it as being the result of his company's failure to thrive in the Internet environment. I smacked my head in disbelief. Clearly, he'd been so moved by his New Radical role that he wanted to spend more of his time doing good. Here's another example: when Stephen Lewis's term as U.N. Special Envoy on HIV/AIDS in Africa ended, he immediately started the Stephen Lewis Foundation to continue this important work: providing care, assisting orphans, supporting grandmothers (whom Lewis calls the "unsung heroes of Africa"), and helping associations of people living with HIV/AIDS. At 69, he has no plans to retire. And Dan O'Brien recently bit off another huge challenge. Sam Hurst—the neighbor who introduced Dan to buffalo—presented him with a proposal for them to buy a ranch together. "I thought about it for 24 hours before heading to the bank." Their new spread is 25,000 acres of roadless pasture "that would take your breath away." And now, instead of resting on his laurels, Dan will be "making payments and paying taxes on this new spread until I die." And he's okay with that.

This idea that we continue to grow and change throughout our lives is something that creative people know to be true. Consider what my beloved Hokusai said about himself: "From the age of 6 I had a mania for drawing the form of things. By the time I was 50, I had published an infinity of designs, but all that I have produced before the age of 70 is not worth taking into account. At 73, I learned a little about the real structure of nature, of animals, plants, birds, fishes, and insects. In consequence, when I am 80, I shall have made more progress; at 90, I shall penetrate the mystery of things; at 100, I shall have reached a marvelous stage; and when I am 110, everything I do, be it a dot or a line, will be alive." Even better, as our roles lead to the "vital engagement" that Mihaly Csikszentmihalyi identified, many new opportunities, more innovation—and creativity—will emerge. We're just getting started.

At this point, New Radicals have figured out the kind of role they want to play. Some can step directly into their new life. For the rest of us, there are some critical pieces of the puzzle to put in place first. We need to find answers to the question: "How do you get there from here?"

Chapter 7

How Do You Get There from Here?

The two million people who have been uprooted by the conflict in Darfur will have great difficulty going home. The UN Environment Program says that desertification, soil erosion, and shrinking rainfall (this last attributed to global warming) means that the region cannot support life as it once did.

—*Financial Times*, June 2007

At this point, the New Radicals have a pretty good sense of where they want to be, but they are not home free. My clients want to know, "How do I get there from here?" The "here" they are referring to is one of two places: either they have decided on a specific role and need help to make it happen or they are still trying to decide and need to find ways to keep the process moving.

So far, New Radicals have been traveling companions, covering similar terrain, and passing common milestones. From this point onward, each one must find his or her our own way. As Victoria Hale puts it: "At a certain point, I realized that for part of this journey I would have blinders on and would have to follow my nose." Which route you take depends on where you are now, what you're going to become, and whether your new role is wildly or mildly radical. In short, we're not just emerging Activists, Entrepreneurs, and Innovators any more, but a million variations on a theme. Even so, there are threads that continue to connect us. What kinds of things might come up as you take the final steps into your new life? You may create a plan, take time to explore new territory, and figure out how to fund your transition.

CREATING YOUR TRANSITION PLAN

The first thing my clients and I talk about as we settle into this new phase is the power of planning: spelling out what they need to do now, breaking this into actionable steps, and establishing a realistic timeline. When I mention the word *plan*, some people immediately flip open their notebooks and dig in. They're pros at this kind of thing, having made endless plans at work, mapped out their careers, and created complex itineraries for family holidays. Others balk. They say they're not interested. They want things to unfold. They wave their hands and say sotto voce, "If it's meant to be . . ." At this point, I have to decide whether or not to persuade them of the value of such an endeavor. Mostly, I try this one little pitch at their hearts.

"Since your wake-up call," I begin quietly, "the idea that life doesn't go on forever has popped up from time to time in our conversations."

They nod.

"It's a simple thing to say, isn't it? Yet, at the same time, difficult to fully grasp."

A little silence hangs between us.

"We may not be 'knocking on heaven's door,'" I say as I look up from my notes, "but we *are* mortal. I don't know about you, but there are lots of things that I didn't do in the first half of my life that I wish I had. And you can be certain that I don't want to be saying the same thing at the age of 80." I take a breath and continue, my whole body getting into the message behind my words. "Or let me put it another way, Hooray! We're alive! There are a million things we want to do, and a zillion ways to help save the world. You've answered the question that is central to this work: 'How do you want to spend the rest of your life?' By all means, stay open to chance, but don't rely on it. Planning simply means that you value something and are willing to invest in it. Let's do everything we can to make it happen!"

I'm sympathetic to this resistance to planning, which I interpret as a denial of aging. It's completely natural—if sometimes a little over the top. For instance, a colleague recently called to talk about my services, saying that she had someone in mind to refer. "He's in his late forties, a senior executive in the financial sector, and doesn't know what to do with the rest of his life." I said I'd be happy to talk to him. "The problem is," she whispered, "I'm not sure he'd want to see a *midlife* coach." At this age—however you describe it!—a plan really is our friend. Even a free spirit like me recognizes this fact. We're pretty good at planning our financial futures. Why not adapt these same principles to how we want to invest—or spend—the rest of our lives?

Clearly, some New Radical roles require more planning than others. For instance, if you're launching a new enterprise or making a wildly radical move, you may need to spend more time strategizing. As you now know, New Radical journeys can stretch out over several years. Nicole Pageau is at one end of the spectrum, with a scant 12 months from her initial inspiration to a new life on a new continent. And Mark Brayne is at the other. For Mark, it was a long, hard slog. "If anyone thinks that this transition is going to be easy, well good luck to them. In my experience, it took years of pain, real soul struggle. I'm 57 this year, and it started when I was 39. It's only now that things are clocking satisfactorily into place, and we're 17 years on." If you're only beginning your New Radical journey, this prospect may seem daunting. Would it help to know that each New Radical discovered that, no matter how long and difficult the voyage, it was worth every moment?

As we discuss the ideas that appear below, my clients incorporate them into their plans.

EXPLORING YOUR NEW WORLD

As we have learned, New Radicals step off the traditional career path. Preparing for new roles can be an extended and complicated process. New Radicals-in-the-making need to understand the world they are about to enter, how it differs from the one they are familiar with, and what it will take for them to be successful in this new environment. This part of the process is about getting it right: ensuring that the role they have in mind is the right fit, that they have the right qualifications, the right attitude, and the right people on their team.

Right Fit

Knowing everything you can about the role you have in mind will help you determine if it's really right for you—if it's aligned with your values, if it makes use of your skills and strengths, and if the environment is one where you will feel comfortable and able to make a difference. We've all made the mistake of assessing something from a distance, only to discover that it's completely different up close. As one client put it, after years of young lieutenants barking at her heels: "Everyone wants to be president, but not too many people want to *do* president." If you intend to become an Activist, for example, talking to people in the field in which you are interested—or, even better, in the precise organization you have in mind—is essential. My clients who have moved from the for-profit to the nonprofit sector have discovered that the new culture is dramatically different from what they were used to. This revelation doesn't surprise Georgina Steinsky-Schwartz. In her role as president and CEO of Imagine Canada (the voice of Canadian charities), Georgina regularly gets asked for advice, and when she does, her message is consistent: do your homework. "Every week some corporate executive invites me out to lunch to talk about how they might switch to working for a nonprofit. I tell them straight out that the social sector is a very different environment, and people need to figure out if they're going to be happy in it." For instance, some people discover that it's difficult to work in a consensus-driven environment. If they are used to being the boss, those conditions can be hard. Georgina continues, "I put it to them directly: in your business you wouldn't dream of launching a product without due diligence; you've got to look before you leap."

Participating in volunteer work is another great way to develop a better understanding of your intended field, and doing so offers the additional advantage of helping you establish credibility at the same time. Remember how Don Stannard-Friel built relationships in the Tenderloin district of San Francisco? Or when Rocco Rossi worked on his friend's mayoral campaign? Carol Menaker, director of communications for the Myelin Repair Foundation, said that this approach worked for her, too: "Volunteering was a great way for me to get my feet wet, and for Scott and the board to get to know me first." In fact, their current COO donated his time at first, and they now have a CFO who comes in once a week as a volunteer.

If, on the other hand, you're going to be an Entrepreneur, make sure you understand what's involved in starting an organization (whether a profit or nonprofit one), and that you have what it takes. Scott Johnson, you'll recall from Chapter 3, realized that he was "uniquely suited" to launch the Myelin Repair Foundation; in addition to a broad range of skills, his background included start-up experience. New Radicals such as Dr. Victoria Hale advises that the New Radical-in-the-making talk with people who have started similar companies or who have necessary information. Victoria met with a range of people when she was starting out. "The Bay Area is full of people who have started biotech companies. I talked to a lot of them." And then, later in her research, she went abroad to understand the opportunities and get to know the players. "For a year and a half I traveled around the world talking to people in global health and infectious diseases."

If you have your heart set on becoming an Innovator, you'll need to figure out how to make the case for what you're proposing to do. You may already have a good sense of whether your organization is open to new ideas. Don Raymond, for instance, knew that the Canada Pension Plan Investment Board's senior management—including the board of directors and CEO—were "in full support of what we were doing." In contrast, Ed Sutt, who, as we learned in Chapter 6, developed the HurriQuake nail, started by taking a good look around. "When I began working at Stanley-Bostitch, 60 percent of our revenues came from fasteners, and there was one engineer working on them, whereas there were about 50 working on tools." He knew he would have to sell the idea of a new type of fastener internally: even in a progressive company looking to enhance its fasteners, everyone thought a nail was just a nail. Next came, in his words, a lot of "skunk work." He completed his assigned projects and developed the new nail on the side. Once the first prototypes were available, interest and enthusiasm understandably began to climb. "We did some internal testing, and even more people got excited. At that point, I lobbied for funding to do some external testing." To Ed, innovation is an incremental process: "You can't climb a mountain in a single step. You have to take tiny ones and keep making the case all the way, and eventually people come around."

Right Qualifications

My clients and I also assess whether they will need new qualifications—such as a degree—in order to assume their role. Climate scientist Ken Caldeira holds a no-nonsense view of this reality: figure out what you need to join the club, and go get it. "The most important thing is to understand what the union card of your new profession is. To a large extent, a Ph.D. is a meaningless piece of paper: it just means you were able to jump through hoops. But that is the union card you need to get a job in my field." On occasion, when novice New Radicals object to the idea of additional education "at this age," I remind them that it's an investment in their future and ask them what they'd rather be doing in 10 years. And—leaving aside good works for the moment—I point out that with two, three, or even four decades of work ahead, it makes sense to put time and money into an education. As one woman said as she made plans to go back to school: "It occurred to me that I would be closer to 60 than 50 when I got my degree. The fact that my 90-year-old aunt still has an active practice in Manhattan helped enormously. I figured had 30 years ahead of me."

Of course, whether they plan to become a psychiatrist, professor, or priest, many New Radicals enthusiastically embrace the idea of learning. And, in addition to traditional institutions, there are lots of innovative new schools and programs to consider. Business schools, in particular, are undergoing a rather dramatic conversion to keep up with the changing demands of their students and the marketplace. Within the schools, a cross-disciplinary approach is emerging, and what they teach is changing, too—ethics, entrepreneurship, and even social entrepreneurship. The last of which is part of what Ray Horton, director of the Social Enterprise Program at Columbia University, calls "a revolution" in business studies. He told the *Financial Times* that Columbia's program has grown from 50 to 400 students and is regularly oversubscribed.

This growing emphasis on social entrepreneurship—essentially, harnessing the principles of business to help drive social change—is good news for New Radicals, as it is a centerpiece of the New Radical movement (Muhammad Yunus and his Grameen Bank being a prime example). Jeff Skoll is the leading social entrepreneur-activist—and a New Radical pioneer. A cofounder of eBay, Skoll now runs a foundation that invests in good works. For instance, he endowed the Skoll Centre for Social Entrepreneurship at Oxford University's Said Business School. Students in what's known as the preeminent program don't simply sit in the classroom, they develop plans that have a positive impact on a specific social problem and work in the field to help make them happen.

For the Next New Radicals, there's another option. In addition to having a wonderfully wacky name, KaosPilots has a reputation as the world's most adventurous alternative business school. Based in Aarhus, Denmark's second-largest city, it offers students a three-year program. Like Skoll Centre students, they select real-world projects, put together a business plan, get the idea off the ground, and solve problems as they arise. Unlike other business schools, a third of the students' time is devoted to development of their "inner pilot"—a kind of emotional intelligence that the school's founders believe leads to creativity and self awareness. And the school has been so successful that it's in the midst of KaosPilots 2.0—an expansion across Europe, with satellite projects popping up in North America.

Speaking of inner pilots, Mark Brayne is now on a first-name basis with his, but this wasn't always the case. In fact, getting to know himself was a long and difficult process—as we heard earlier, his transformation took place over several decades. His career started out in the usual way: on graduating from university, he was offered a job and worked as a journalist at Reuters and, later, the BBC World Service for nearly 30 years. During one of our early-morning trans-Atlantic phone calls, he told me that the working atmosphere of journalism was an enormously rich one: "I knew some of the most interesting people on the planet, was changing posts every three or four years, immersing myself in different cultures, and learning new languages, which I adore." Despite it all, he was deeply unhappy. "All the while, there was a drumbeat going on inside: 'This is not me, this is not me' . . . I knew that something was profoundly wrong. And I just put a brave face on it."

Mark's wake-up call was particularly dramatic. It was 1989, which he describes as "a global year of transition." He went to Romania to cover the violent revolution that overthrew Central Europe's last communist ruler, Nicolae Ceausescu. He arrived in Bucharest on the twenty-third of December, while there was still shooting in the streets, but before Ceausescu had been executed. It was an absolutely terrifying experience and yet an extraordinarily moving one. "On the streets in the days that followed, there was an explosion of love and brotherhood like I'd never known. And my heart was blasted wide open as a result of this experience." Taking the train out of Bucharest, heading home to an unhappy marriage, in despair about his career, he sat down next to a woman, and fell instantly and madly in love. And all of these things coming together woke him up. "It was the big turning point. I see now that a classic midlife crisis had been brewing—consciousness waiting to break through that had piled up over 40 years. And then the secret was out. Not just the affair, but the misery of my entire life."

While a series of crises might have sent others into therapy, Mark was seized by the idea that he should study the discipline: "I rang a place I liked the look of, and asked them to send me some material. And they said, 'would you like an interview?' and suggested that very afternoon. It was that simple." He laughed at the memory. Mark soon signed up for a transpersonal psychology training course (leading to a master's degree) and, later, entered therapy himself. All the while, he was working at the BBC and his marriage was unraveling. It seemed inevitable that one career would end and a completely different one would begin. But, as he told us earlier, he eventually realized that what he needed to do was "circle back in" and bring things he was learning from psychology to bear on journalism.

Before Mark became a New Radical Activist, he was an Innovator. While studying, he helped establish the BBC's first confidential counseling service "at a time when journalists in Britain were hostile to the idea of revealing personal emotion." And now he had a new idea to suggest: that the entire industry needed to be sensitized to trauma awareness and emotional literacy. The initial reaction was not good. "It was, 'Oh, no! Not Brayne and his emotions again!'" But this time he had his research and a respected organization to back him up. He'd begun working with the Dart Center—a global network of journalists, journalism educators, and health professionals. The center's goals were in line with what Mark wanted to do: improve coverage of trauma, conflict, and tragedy, and address the consequences of such coverage for journalists. The BBC gave Mark a two-month window to get the project off the ground; coverage of the war in Iraq extended it to nine.

Mark was particularly interested in what happens to journalists and their coworkers. When he was working on his master's degree, he discovered Dr. Anthony Feinstein, who had done pioneering work on the experience of frontline reporters and camera crews. Feinstein found that those with 15 years on the front lines—reporting on wars, earthquakes, and the like—had above-average levels of anxiety. In fact, about one in four of these journalists—the same number as combat veterans—had experienced full-blown posttraumatic stress disorder (PTSD). And the pressures on journalists are increasing—more reporters were killed on the job in 2006 than ever before. (When I wrote this section, BBC journalist Alan Johnston had been held captive in Gaza for more than 100 days. He has since been freed.)

And Mark was also concerned with how reporters approach their work: "There tends to be a fair bit of unthinking macho toughness—aspects of which are needed to get the job done, of course." He wanted to help shift the culture toward something more rounded, reasoning that if journalists understood trauma better, they would be more insightful and compassionate in their reporting. "Trauma is 60 to 70 percent of the news. People who cover sport know everything about the game. Why shouldn't people who cover conflict zones understand trauma?"

There's also a robust business case to be made for introducing such notions into newsrooms. Programs that help people understand trauma—and cope with their own—will ensure that journalists perform at their best for longer periods of time. And then there's the duty of care. Each media organization has policies in place to ensure that staff don't injure themselves, yet there are less visible kinds of harm to consider. "Emotional safety is just as important as physical. If one of your reporters or camera people gets PTSD, it raises the issue of liability."

Today, Mark has hung up his reporter's boots. He works as a psychotherapist with individuals, journalists, and news organizations in London and across Europe, and he is the European director of the Dart Center. In fact, it was through the center that Mark met his second wife, Sue, which gives his story a particularly happy ending. "We both had previous marriages and full lives, and when we married, I said it was an unusually direct example of Dart Center support for posttrauma recovery."

Right Attitude

As Mark discovered—"not Brayne and his emotions again!"—our passions are not always welcomed with open arms. As we learned in Chapter 3, in the earliest days of the New Radicals movement—just a few years ago—there was considerable wariness between the pioneers and the people they sought to help. The natural skepticism of people from other sectors wasn't helped by the fact that enthusiastic New Radicals kept appearing on the doorsteps of hospitals, schools, and charities claiming that they were here to save them. Understandably, the smart, savvy people inside these institutions were uncomfortable with such enthusiasm, no matter how well intentioned. Rocco Rossi, one of the first to cross the divide between the corporate and nonprofit worlds, was unequivocal about the dangers: "We fool ourselves into thinking we're God's gift to the nonprofits. That the moment we apply business analysis and tools, we'll take everything to a new level." When considering one's attitude in our New Radical role, humility, it seems, is the operative word.

Even once you're ensconced, it's important to find a balance between what you have been used to and the way the new environment operates. When Verizon executive Bruce S. Gordon became CEO of the National Association for the Advancement of Colored People (NAACP)—the first outsider to assume this role—it was a clear signal that the board felt he could complement the strengths and skills that already existed in the organization. When Rocco and I talked about this issue, he acknowledged that it can be tricky to find a happy medium between two worlds: "I certainly stumbled in my first months on the job as I struggled to introduce new ideas and hold on to what was important about the existing way of doing things. I'm glad I didn't succumb, though, to the Stockholm syndrome [that is, identifying and sympathizing with the people holding you down]. Because, in that dynamic tension, new growth happened."

Former Olympian Johann Koss also had difficulty adjusting, until he figured out what was going on. Although he was in a leadership role, the territory was unfamiliar: "As someone who had been quite successful, and then to enter a new world . . . I had to recognize that I was not starting out at the same level. I lost my feeling of mastery at first, and that was deeply frustrating."

In general, I suggest that my accomplished, confident clients approach their new role—whether Activist, Entrepreneur, or Innovator—with what's known as "beginner's mind." There's a Zen saying that, in the mind of the beginner infinite possibilities exist, while in the mind of the expert there are few. (If the men and women I'm talking to look at me like I'm crazy, I suggest instead that they try to remember what it was like to be in Grade 9.) If you're still questioning whether humility is essential, consider this. A recent study shows that it is the best tool for learning. Those who think they know the least ask more questions, do more research, and prove to be more effective than those who think they know it all.

Right People

As we've discovered, getting the right people on your team is vitally important. At this stage, New Radicals are concerned with two kinds of people: those who can help them begin their new role, and those who will help make it a success. When New Radicals did their research—"what does the world need?"—some of the individuals they met became part of their network. I suggest to my clients that now is the time to call on those people again (as well as to add new contacts), as those individuals might be able to provide specific information, and even help New Radicals-in-the-making step into their new roles. Suzanne Seggerman, who met people at her first game developers' conference who have since become an essential part of her world, said that "in the beginning there was just a tiny group of us interested in games for nonentertainment purposes. We were all doing it in isolation—garage developers, you know?" Each year, the group expands a little more. Now there is a whole community, sharing ideas and information.

New Radicals also need people to help them get their new organizations off the ground. Sometimes, they had to work hard to find people who were open to new ideas and ready to make a move. Scott Johnson, for instance, talked about how difficult it was to assemble his team. The scientists he was interested in told him that the Myelin Repair Foundation's innovative research approach was appealing, but also scary—it was completely contrary to the system they knew so well. "It was so intellectually challenging, though, that, one by one, they came on board. I think being able to brainstorm with other brilliant people they respected made a difference." It helps that they are New Radicals, too. "One of them said, 'For the first 20 years of my career I never wanted to see someone with a disease. I wanted to do pure science.'" And now he had reached a point where he wanted to actively help people.

Victoria Hale made sure to emphasize the value of her worldwide team, noting that the Institute for OneWorld Health succeeded because everyone played a role—that it really took a global village: "We needed everyone from government to pharmaceutical companies, to field workers to nonprofits, from the technical people to those who are sensitive to the culture and values of the people in the countries where we're working." The founder is important, but that person isn't everything, can't be everything.

"The founder needs people to work with her. And New Radical organizations need both."

You could say that people are David Simms's raison d'etre. As mentioned earlier, he is managing partner of Bridgestar, an innovative firm that is helping nonprofits find the talent they need. When we sat down together, it was soon clear that David, age 50, comes with precisely the right credentials for his New Radical role: "I've actually had two careers, one paid, and the other volunteer."

After earning several degrees—management technology at the University of Pennsylvania and business and law at Harvard—David joined Bain & Company, a consulting firm that does Fortune 500 strategy globally. "It was a wonderful way to cut my teeth and learn the ins and outs of business and how to think about strategy from a for-profit perspective." Next, he was a White House Fellow, and worked for the U.S. deputy secretary of state. Eager to try his hand in different sectors, he left government to run his own venture capital firm, then led a turnaround at the American Red Cross in Baltimore before moving to the corporate sector yet again to manage a number of start-ups for MBNA America. It was a good life: challenging and rewarding. And while he was completely fulfilled by his volunteer work—with Opportunity International, which provides microloans to the poorest people in 29 developing countries—he knew it was time for a more meaningful career. "That mission-driven part of me said, 'This isn't what you're called to do.' And so I put out the word that I was ready to change what I was doing for a living."

In a wonderful example of synchronicity, at just that moment someone was looking for him. The nonprofit arm of Bain & Company, Bridgespan, had been applying the same strategic principles that they had learned over the years to the nonprofit sector and were doing fabulously well, with offices in Boston, San Francisco, and New York. But Bridgespan's management was struggling with how to address the issue of leadership in the charitable sector. "You can have great strategy, and even great capital, but in the absence of great leadership, you're not going to get the results you want." At that particular point, Bridgespan was looking for what they called a "bridger"—someone who had experience in both the for-profit and nonprofit worlds—to head its new talent division, Bridgestar. With perfect timing, David added his name to Bain's database. "The folks at Bain run a service for their alumni. You can put your CV [curriculum vitae] into their system, and they'll try to match you with opportunities." He took the call, and the rest is history.

We circle back to the issue of the shortage of good talent, which I've seen time and again in my own research, because David wanted to emphasize one point: there are good people working in the nonprofit sector now. "People in mission-driven organizations have to operate, most often, in resource-constrained environments where the executive director spends half his time out raising funds. It's an incredibly difficult job, and there are definitely people in the sector who do it brilliantly." We agreed that it's also true that more people—and fresh thinking—are urgently needed.

Bridgestar has been working with New Radicals for a number of years, and it is beginning to hear from the Next New Radicals, too. "We're now seeing people at about [the age of] 30 or so, a few years after business school, who've paid down their school debt, and are saying things like, 'I don't want to wait another

15 or 20 years to do important work, I want to make the transition now.'"

David feels blessed to have the good fortune of working with a group of people who have chosen to serve society in this way. "Everyone who works with us could be making more money, sometimes much more money, in the private sector." Instead of creating wealth, they are making a world of difference. And he says that it's only just begun: "I agree with what you're seeing, Julia. We think that the magnitude of workplace change that's coming will astonish us all."

FUNDING YOUR TRANSITION

Whenever I speak publicly about the New Radicals, someone always raises the issue of money. It's clear that some high-profile people doing good works have the resources to do whatever they want. People want to know: "Is it really possible for me?" Absolutely. In fact, this is one of the central ideas of this book—inspiring you to see that ordinary people like you and I can become New Radicals, too.

The question, it seems to me, actually has two parts: "How do I fund the transition?" and "Can I make enough to live?" The first question is relatively simple to answer. While some New Radicals have resources they can draw on—such as investments or an early retirement package—the vast majority do not. Instead, they juggle two lives: they continue their existing career while preparing for their new role. Mark Brayne is just one example; he continued to work full time while studying. "I was putting in a 50-hour workweek at the BBC. In at 8 a.m. for a nine o'clock editorial meeting, helping to run the European language services, 12 of them, working flat out from eight till half past six, with my psychotherapy and training on top." My own story is cut from the same cloth. For four years, I continued to run my first business while working hard to launch a new practice, all while researching and writing this book.

For New Radicals starting new ventures, capitalization issues are similar to those faced by any other start-up or charity. But when a New Radical venture was highly unusual—"the world's first *what*?"—things got more complicated. Victoria Hale, for instance, ran into difficulty with the American tax department (the Internal Revenue Service, or IRS), which thought that "nonprofit pharmaceutical company" was an oxymoron. The IRS wanted to know why a very profitable industry needed a nonprofit firm. Victoria relied on two answers: need and precedent. "OneWorld Health talked about how the beneficiaries were not American and are very poor. And our firm reminded them that, in the '60s and '70s, when private broadcasting was lucrative, the IRS had allowed a television station and radio network—PBS and NPR—to exist as nonprofits." The government agreed there was a parallel and that a need was being met. OneWorld Health got its approval.

The second part of the question—"Can I make enough to live?"—is more complicated. First, let me reiterate that New Radicals are working for pay. The vast majority need to continue to support themselves financially; these people are not volunteers. "I have to earn a living," is how Bill Duggan, age 48, put it when I reached him in Sri Lanka. Bill now works as field director of the plantation communities project for the World University Service of Canada. “We have one child, and we’re about to become a family of five—my wife is pregnant with twins.”

Some New Radicals intend to make a lot of money—Entrepreneurs in particular (like Vinod Khosla, mentioned in Chapter 5). Innovators who continue in their original roles may continue to earn high salaries. For many New Radicals, though, it’s a different story. Activists, as David Simms pointed out, don’t make as much money as their peers in the for-profit world. Don Raymond took a cut in pay when he left Wall Street to work for the Canada Pension Plan Investment Board. Wendy Kopp made a similar point about her Teach for America recruits. However, the gap between the sectors is not as wide as it once was, and it will continue to narrow. Columbia professor Ray Horton told the *Financial Times* that the average annual salary for Columbia’s business school graduates working in the not-for-profit sector is about $90,000. While it may not be as much money as they’d earn in the private sector, it’s enough. And here’s what’s at the heart of this question: most New Radicals told me that money is no longer their primary motivator and that they happily traded lifestyle for meaning. John Wood is a great example. Once a rising star at Microsoft, he quit his job to bring books and schooling to underserved communities around the world. How did he cope with the associated drop in income? He stopped looking at his bank statements each month because his dwindling balance depressed him, and he learned to ignore the ads for luxury goods he could no longer afford. “I reminded myself every day that what matters most in life is whether I’m happy and serving some greater purpose. I learned to stop using money as my metric.”

One day, while thinking about all the stories I'd heard of people struggling mightily toward their dreams, I began to wonder if having considerable resources might even work against us. Might it be yet another example of the "uses of adversity"? If I hadn't had to struggle, would I have given up long ago? If Ed didn't need a job at the wind facility to finance his degree, would he have gotten the experience that led to the HurriQuake nail? If Mark hadn't continued working while studying to become a psychotherapist, would he have made the connection that gave him his brilliant new career? And might Leonard Cohen, Canadian singer-songwriter, poet, and novelist, be the modern-day equivalent of Hokusai—might his greatest contribution emerge as a result of his having to go back to work? (In his seventies, Cohen was astonished to discover that the money he had set aside throughout his career had been embezzled.) New Radical Entrepreneur Ron Dembo had clearly been thinking along the same lines. He started his first company with no money and is trying to simulate the same conditions with his new firm, Zerofootprint. "It's nice to have resources, but not having money makes you work much harder and be more innovative."

The important lesson, I suggest, is not to let money stand in the way of what we really want to do. In her early sixties, Nicole Pageau got rid of her possessions and moved to another country. "I sold everything I could, like my old car, and some things from my apartment. Combined with what I raised at a small dinner, it added up to $5,000. With that, two suitcases, and a box of toys for the children, I left for Rwanda."

FINDING YOUR WAY

New Radical pioneers discovered that the path was—as Victoria Hale noted in the opening of this chapter—uncharted and that they had to find their own way forward. As this movement evolves, this groping in the dark will become less necessary. As more of us become New Radicals, we'll reach out to others in transition, sharing ideas and information. Support systems will be established: I predict huge growth in New Radical mentoring. In fact, resources are already appearing—as Bridgestar and the two schools I have mentioned in this chapter indicate. (Other sources I share with my clients are listed in the Resources section at the back of this book.)

Before leaving this part of the process behind, I encourage my clients to do two things: First, they need to consider their emerging abilities. Just as new possibilities appeared on their horizon as we worked together, they have gained new insights into themselves. In particular, we talk about how adversity can lead to personal development. What capabilities have risen to the surface—"I didn't know I had that in me!"—and what do we need to incorporate into their view of themselves and to put into play? Drew McManus, who cofounded Bring Light with Melissa Dyrdahl, discovered that his New Radical role changed him and how he operates. Having worked in big companies for so many years, he had gotten really good at consensus: preparing a presentation and shopping the idea around for a week to build support. "The other day, I realized that I now make a hundred decisions a day, all by myself." As a result, things move at a faster clip. "If you'd asked me six months ago if we'd be close to going to beta, I would have said 'no way!' And yet we are. It's a fantastic feeling."

Second, new New Radicals need to keep the connection to their deepest selves and their mission alive. Some people are surprised at this notion, expecting that, well, now that they are New Radicals, it will just happen naturally. I remind them that they are likely to be as busy as ever and that it's still possible to be swept off course. I offer David Simms as an example of just how full a New Radical's schedule can be. When we chatted, it emerged that the day before was David's fiftieth birthday. I asked him how he spent it. "I woke up at 4:30 in the morning, got on a plane, flew to Milwaukee, worked on a project with a big national network, and arrived home at 9 p.m. to have a birthday cake with my family." In my consulting practice, I encourage emerging New Radicals to think of how they might maintain the connection. For instance, to continue the finance analogy, might they periodically review and refresh their plans? Some talk about building in regular time for reflection (like Rocco Rossi). Others say they'll reassess what they're doing periodically so that they continue to evolve (like Jamie Kennedy). And some say they'll use the New Radicals credo—or create one that has personal meaning—and refer to it often.

Stephen Lewis believes that a moral code is an essential part of our new lives: "I think it is extremely important as a New Radical to have a set of principles, a set of convictions from which you do not swerve. The most effective advocates are those whose principles are known and understood. These principles give you an anchor against which to measure your own efforts and the response of others."

And it is this conviction and clarity—about who we are and how we want to live in this world—that carry us into the last phase of the process and help us answer the second-to-last question: "How do you make a name for yourself?"

Chapter 8

How Do You Make a Name for Yourself?

One of the great wonders of the natural world—the flight of huge clouds of monarch butterflies migrating across North America to the mountains of Mexico—is under threat. For years, scientists have warned that GM [genetically modified] crops and illegal logging were destroying the butterflies' habitat. And projects to protect them are failing.

—*The Guardian Weekly*, June 2007

"I used to be the next president of the United States."

Chances are you know whose line that is. It's one that goes down well with Al Gore's adoring audiences. And it speaks volumes about this New Radical pioneer. In a single phrase he's saying that, like us, he had a midlife wake-up call, reassessed his life, looked into his heart and at the problems of our world, and charted a new course. Gore now has star power of a different kind. He sells out his shows—touring with his Oscar award-winning documentary, *An Inconvenient Truth*—like a rock star. He has a new nickname, "the Goracle." And, just as this book was going to press, was awarded the Nobel Peace Prize. Why has Gore been so successful in his New Radical role? One reason is because he developed a personal brand that resonates with the public. I hesitate to call it branding, because in some quarters the word is so loaded. But that's really what this is. Individuals like Gore are doing what companies have done for years: developing identities to help market themselves.

To me, the real beauty of branding is that it is a kind of sophisticated shorthand. Done well, it is a clear, concise answer to three related questions: "Who are you?" "What do you do?" and "What can you do for me?"

(Product) Red is one example of branding that New Radicals and I often discuss, as it hit the marketplace just as this movement was getting underway. Founded by Bono and Bobby Shiver, chairman of DATA (debt, AIDS, trade, Africa), the campaign brings together a number of corporate partners. Each licenses the Red name for its specially made Red products and donates a percentage of the sales of these products to the Global Fund (which, by the way, underwrites the work of Dr. Mark Grabowsky, whose story appears in Chapter 3). (Product) Red says here's who we are: some of the world's most trusted brands, including Motorola, Emporio Armani, Gap, American Express, Converse, and Apple. It says here's what we do: we've created this umbrella campaign that allows us to leverage our distinctive corporate assets to make money *and* provide a sustainable flow of income to the Global Fund. And here's what we can do for you: give you a way to purchase a product (for the same price as a non-Red version), knowing that some of the money is going to do good works. Gap, for instance, donates 50 percent of the profits from its Red line.

My clients and I talk about (Product) Red because it mirrors what emerging New Radicals are about to do. Now that they have a good grasp of what they have to offer and a clear idea about how they can make a difference, they are ready to make a name for themselves. We're not starting from scratch, of course. Like you, my clients have established reputations. Our task is to create a new identity on this solid foundation—one that makes it clear why this particular New Radical-in-the-making is the ideal person for the role. This part of our work together is always important, but it's critical if my client intends to make more than the simplest shift—if he is leaving corporate life and applying for a job with a nongovernmental organization (NGO) in Bolivia, for instance, or if she has decided to give up dentistry so she can grow green oil (also known as ethanol). And it can be particularly helpful if they are trying to win hearts and minds inside their organization—persuading the powers that be precisely how they will make a world of difference.

I tell my clients that I can't promise them a standing ovation, but I do guarantee that their chances of successfully landing—or launching—their New Radical role will be greatly enhanced if they follow some simple principles. What's more, they'll be delighted to discover that all the work they have done so far provides the information they need to answer the three questions that form the heart of a brand: "Who are you?" "What do you do?" and "What can you do for me?"

WHO ARE YOU?

Branding experts use this first question to get at the essence of the brand—that is, what's fundamental and unchanging. They call this the "core identity." I suggest that New Radicals think about it as their character. We reflect back on what we have learned about our strengths, our values, and what we stand for. Answering this question is often a deeply moving experience: we are putting into words what we know about the deepest parts of ourselves, and we are aware that our answers mean a great deal to us and will also matter to others. As we have discussed, New Radical organizations are going out of their way to find and keep the right kind of people—those with character—and this trend will only increase.

For many New Radicals, these details form a prominent part of their identity. Wendy Kopp's passionate belief in equality of education is a good example, as is Dr. Mark Grabowsky's utilitarian ideal. And Dr. Victoria Hale told me that, after she started the Institute for OneWorld Health, people remarked that she had been talking about making medicines for the diseases of the poor for more than a decade—so others saw it as part of who she was long before she had completely acknowledged it herself. And many New Radicals discovered that having a clearly defined and well-recognized character brought opportunities their way. When Stephen Lewis became the U.N. special envoy on HIV/AIDS in Africa, it was widely reported that the newly created post was the result of his lifetime of humanitarian work, including a role with UNICEF. He quickly made a new name for himself as a vigorous and vocal champion of the cause. The world noticed, and the honors poured in, including *Time* magazine's list of the world's 100 most influential people. (A classic New Radical, Stephen would undoubtedly say that such honors matter only as far as they help him continue his work.)

Not surprisingly, some New Radicals found that their emerging self and their existing reputation dovetailed to create the ideal calling card. Melissa Dyrdahl, age 50, has already shared an important realization with us: that the charitable component of her corporate position was tiny relative to the amount of satisfaction it was delivering. In response, she started doing volunteer work in the nonprofit community. "I was helping organizations think strategically about marketing."

As her unhappiness with her current career intensified, Melissa became aware of a long-buried part of herself: an entrepreneurial spirit that was, she says, "dying to get out." One day, she and Drew McManus, age 40, another Adobe alumni, met to have lunch. They had worked together on dozens of projects over the years at several different companies—Melissa on the marketing side, and Drew in technology. They respected and trusted each other enormously. At the restaurant, they poured out their frustrations and longings to each other. And then they did something that seemed like a completely natural next step and breathtakingly bold at the same time. They decided to start a company together. "By the end of the meal, we had sketched out a rough plan." Their idea was a Web-based service that would help nonprofit organizations market themselves to new donors. It would also incorporate an innovative social network component, so that groups of donors could band together to support causes and thereby magnify their impact. And they would call this new venture Bring Light.

In terms of making it happen, their timing couldn't have been better. Drew was about to take a long-anticipated leave of absence. He spent it doing research, looking at the sociological and psychological aspects of giving, and the philanthropic trends among those people labeled Generations X and Y (Gen X and Y) whom they saw as their primary—though by no means only—target audience. Drew also looked into the growth of online contributions. Today, only about 5 percent of donations are done via the Web—a drop in the bucket compared to shopping and banking—and that giving generally occurs around the time things like disasters happen. Yet Americans give $200 billion a year to charities. "We realized that we were on the cusp of something huge." They also looked at the competition and discovered that there were a lot of what are known as charity directories—a potential donor chooses dogs, for instance, and is presented with a long list of nonprofit groups that help canines. The idea is to pick one and make your donation. To New Radical Entrepreneurs reared in Silicon Valley, this method didn't seem terribly creative, nor did it make the best use of the medium. Drew put it this way, "It's not very interesting, and it's definitely one way: you just put your money in a slot."

Their research showed that people—particularly younger people—wanted to be engaged and to know what happens to their money. So, Bring Light was designed to differ from what's out there in several important ways. Donors are presented with very specific choices. For instance, let's say that the Humane Society needs to buy sturdy beds for its dogs. Visitors to the site will discover details about the dogs, the beds, how many are needed, and how the money will be used. In addition to making a donation, people can visit any time, comment, and keep track of what's happening with the pooches and their pillows. And they can also get others involved, as a way to enhance their efforts. Drew continued: "They might think, 'I've got $20 to give. Maybe I could get 20 friends together, and we could really make something happen.'" Donors realize they can make a bigger difference with little extra effort—and have fun in the bargain.

While Drew had a dedicated period of time to invest in Bring Light's research and development, for Melissa it was a long, slow start. Still working full time, she could meet with people in the nonprofit sector to talk about this new enterprise only in her spare time. She admits that "there were lots of meetings over dinner or glasses of wine on the weekend." Plus, although Bring Light wasn't competing with Melissa and Drew's employer, they wanted to be really careful to signal that they were still committed to Adobe, so Melissa chose nonprofits that were new to her. Despite their well-intentioned efforts, word got out: the nonprofit sector is a small, closely knit community. Melissa and Drew's goal was to do a beta test of their site with six or eight organizations, and soon twice that number had signed up. This encouraging early response helped them believe that they were on the right track and that a second vote of confidence was just around the corner.

As they developed their business plan, Melissa asked Adobe's senior director of worldwide research and planning, David Mills, to review it. He would take a strict market analysis approach—she described him as a deeply analytical thinker—and if he liked it, the partners would know they were really onto something. And he did. "David came back and said that he thought it was a great idea. Even better, that he'd love to be involved."

Bring Light's name was Melissa's idea. How she came up with it says a lot about her nature. At the end of her corporate career, sitting in conference rooms, day after day, she felt as though she were holding onto a big, black ball, when what she really wanted to be doing was the opposite. "I wanted to be holding a ball of glowing light, so that I could spread hope." It's standard practice in the software world to give projects code names, and Bring Light was theirs. Funny thing about code names—developers often become attached to these temporary monikers, and they have to be weaned off them when the product is finally launched. This time, it worked in reverse. People really liked the name, and they didn't want it to change. "As we went into the marketplace, people convinced us that we should keep it. So, Bring Light it is."

WHAT DO YOU DO?

What we do is known in branding circles as our "extended identity." In other words, what we have learned—our knowledge and expertise. For New Radical's purposes, this is about our experiences, skills, and resources. In a word, it's about our capacity. Clients often feel pretty terrific when answering this question. They are proud of what they have accomplished. And they are excited about being able to leverage these credentials in fresh ways, as they begin to establish a New Radical reputation for themselves. For instance, Mary Gordon's decades of experience in education gave her the credibility she needed to start Roots of Empathy. Stephon Marbury knew that his "expensive shoes don't matter" message meant more coming from someone who plays for the National Basketball Association (NBA). And Mark Brayne had 30 years of journalism under his belt plus the added weight of the Dart Center when he broached the idea of a program designed to help modulate the journalistic culture within the BBC.

And here's where the potential of this generation really starts to come into view. At midlife, we have significant advantages over our younger selves, including in terms of access. You'll recall how doors swung open for New Radical pioneer—and Silicon Valley success story—Vinod Khosla as he made the rounds with his green energy presentation. Zerofootprint's Ron Dembo told me that his experience was similar: that having people know his name and what he'd accomplished was enormously useful as he tried to get his new enterprise off the ground: "I had created this successful company, Algorithmics, and found that I could leverage my past as a risk specialist. People would listen to me when I started talking about my new idea. I could get in doors that would never have opened otherwise."

At one level, "What do you do?" is a simple question, often the first thing we ask on meeting someone new. But it's a query that must have given Paul Gillespie pause in some circles. One can imagine that his answer, "I work in the sex crimes unit of the Toronto police force," would make some people blanch.

Paul, age 47, was with the Toronto Police Service for nearly 30 years, the last six as part of the Toronto Police Sex Crimes

Unit. There were 60 men and women in all in the unit, divided into three sections. Paul was the officer in charge of the Child Exploitation Section: 17 people whose only job was to conduct Internet child porn investigations, the largest such force in North America. It wasn't always that way; they started out small. "We gradually made the case for a larger group."

Headlines certainly helped. The first flurry of attention came when Paul wrote to Bill Gates expressing frustration about how ill equipped police were to battle the flood of Internet child abuse. "He responded immediately." And how! Microsoft ponied up $10 million, and the Child Exploitation Tracking System (CETS) is the result. A computer software program that supports more effective intelligence-led investigations, it allows law enforcement officers to collaborate and share information. The system was designed with input from hundreds of officers from all over the world. And Microsoft was an active partner, too. "They were with us all the way, and went back to the drawing board again and again until we came up with very sophisticated software." Today, CETS is in place in Canada, and it is being deployed around the world, including Australia, Brazil, Britain, Chile, Colombia, Indonesia, Italy, Spain, and the United States. The second round of media attention came when Paul's team had a major success with a case. The team was able to use technology to trace a child to Raleigh, North Carolina, within 36 hours. The innovation was to take the child out of the image while showing everything else in the room. "Now this image analysis technology can be used again and again."

It's abundantly clear in talking to Paul that the advent of the Internet changed the way police intercept these criminals. He likens it to the wild west: there are no borders, no jurisdictions, no international law. When police looked at a crime scene photograph—"which is what child pornography is"—they had no idea if it had been taken down the street or on the other side of the world. So Paul's team decided to follow the leads wherever they might go, working with police officers in dozens of countries. In doing so, they knew they were really pushing the limits—as municipal police officers, getting paid by City of Toronto residents, and being expected to enforce the law in Toronto. But for this team, they did what mattered most: "We ignored the jurisdiction and followed the trail."

It's difficult subject matter to come to terms with, including the size of the problem. There are an estimated 14 *million* Web sites that display child abuse images! In 2004, in Toronto alone, Paul's team recovered 3 million pictures from the computers of people they arrested. Even today, what stays with Paul is the content. He wants to disabuse me of any notion that these are children frolicking in bathtubs full of bubbles: "These are brutal, hard-core images and movies. The child from North Carolina was in the hands of the worst kind of offender, a specialist in what's known as 'hurt core.'" Apparently sexually assaulting a child isn't enough for these criminals; pain must be inflicted as well.

Paul's passion for the protection of children is in ample evidence when we speak. Today, he works as both a private consultant and as the head of a nonprofit organization: the Kids' Internet Safety Alliance (KINSA). He shifted to his new role for reasons that might appear contradictory—a kind of burnout coupled with a desire to do more—but are perfectly in keeping with the New Radical profile. "To be honest, I just couldn't look at the images any more, or listen to the children screaming. I knew

I wanted to continue working on these issues, and this seemed like the natural next step." He's working with Microsoft to take the CETS database to police around the world. And KINSA will set up a training center to instruct investigators, especially those from poorer countries. "Eventually, we hope to take the show on the road, traveling to as many countries as possible."

More needs to happen, and Paul knows it. He wants to bring a crime so distasteful that most of us prefer to ignore it out of the closet. Even better, he'd like to see someone famous take it on. "No one wants to talk about Internet child abuse. No celebrities want to attach their names to it, either. What we need is [someone who does] what Elizabeth Taylor did for AIDS—someone who's not afraid to stand up."

WHAT CAN YOU DO FOR ME?

In branding terms, your "potential identity" is what you might do now or the direction you might take in the future. This fits perfectly for New Radicals, who have been thinking about what the world needs and how they might help. At this juncture, clients often "get" it: they see that they really do have what it takes to do what they once only dreamed of. Today, I know of hundreds of New Radicals who are answering this question in astonishing ways. Here are three very different examples.

New Radical pioneer Jeff Skoll is, as we have seen already, involved in numerous good works. This year, he partnered with Silicon Valley entrepreneur Kamran Elahian to do something in one of the world's most troubled regions. Together, they launched the Gandhi Project—dubbing Richard Attenborough's epic film *Gandhi* into Arabic, and distributing it in the Palestinian territories and other strife-torn parts of the Arab world. (The night before I wrote this section there was an item on *BBC World News* that showed passive resistance in Gaza. Looking at those brave people lying on their backs on the streets, flashing peace symbols even as Hamas shot at them, I wondered if they had seen the movie.)

Sheila Watt-Cloutier has a particularly innovative—and poignant—answer to this question. It's no secret that the polar regions are in trouble: temperatures are rising faster there than anywhere else on the planet. But few people realize that it's not just polar bears that are affected by the change in polar climate. The way of life for thousands of people scattered across northern Alaska, Canada, Greenland, and Russia may be disappearing forever. Sheila, an Inuit born within the Arctic Circle, has done something astonishing for her people: she has made what's going on a human rights issue. She petitioned the Inter-American Commission on Human Rights, seeking a declaration that "emissions of greenhouse gases that are destroying the Inuit way of life are a violation of human rights." In recognition of this New Radical approach, Sheila was nominated—along with Al Gore—for a Nobel Peace Prize.

New Radical Activist Tony Leighton understands this "making a name" business better than most. It's in his blood. For more than 30 years, he's made his living as a writer—first for magazines, and then as a business writer for some of North America's largest organizations. His New Radical role began when he became aware that developers in the small city where he lives were influencing the politicians, and he felt compelled to act. "They'd swept a perfectly good government out of office, replacing it with one that was so baldly pro-developer it was a disgrace. I decided I had to do something." He gathered a group of like-minded people to encourage local citizens to become interested in issues that affected their lives and get them out to vote. Thanks to a team of professionals like Tony, they were able to achieve something extraordinary. "Marketing for a company is taking fairly complicated and maybe even dull information and making it interesting so that people read it, and compelling so that they act." They did this for the civic campaign, laying out the facts, and giving people the language they needed to go out and start talking about things like waste management, heritage preservation, and land speculation. And it worked. People got excited. There was a real buzz as conversations spread out across his city. "All of a sudden, everyone was having animated discussions about local politics as if talking about sports or their favorite TV show. It was astonishing." And it was effective: a new council was elected with a solid majority.

"Power to the people" is an idea that is coming back into vogue—with a "positive, constructive, hopeful" twist. Patty Johnson is a fine example of this principle in action, only her story is about helping resuscitate indigenous skills. When Patty, age 46, and I talked, it was immediately clear that "What can you do for me?" was at the top of her agenda. Her New Radical role was fueled by deep dissatisfaction with the way the multibillion-dollar global handicrafts business works. A lot of these objects, she believes, are degradations of the skills that people once used to make things for themselves. They meet a new kind of need now, including giving tourists something to spend their money on. One day, Patty wondered whether there wasn't a way to do things differently: "to produce high-quality goods that are a fusion of north and south—northern sensibilities and southern skills." The short answer is yes. Patty's North South Project is creating sophisticated hybrid design products, winning awards, and growing in all directions.

She began her journey as a designer, and then as a consultant for the Canadian International Development Agency (CIDA), working with 14 factories in Guyana. In the back of her mind, always, was this idea that there had to be a way to make beautifully designed, high-quality things that would sell in North America and Europe. The transformation from designer-consultant to New Radical Entrepreneur wasn't an easy one. She began by clarifying what she was bringing to the table, including design skills she had honed over the years, as well as knowledge of and access to northern markets. Then she started to identify people with whom she might like to work. In particular, one woman stood out, an innovator by the name of Jocelyn Dow. Patty says that Jocelyn "was doing great things with a vine that grows in the rainforest, a sustainable alternative to traditional caning." Patty talked to potential partners about what their contributions might be, including knowledge of ancient traditions, local materials, and regional design vocabularies. All the while, she was very clear about one thing: these would be true partnerships. Traditionally, craftspeople in developing countries—whether as a branch plant for a northern manufacturer or as part of the souvenir industry—haven't been treated well, or paid fairly. This time, it would be different. "I was going to bring an egalitarian attitude. I was not going to be a 'middleman' who had come to buy their stuff."

On this basis, she moved forward. She talked to Jocelyn about doing something together, and the Guyanese businesswoman eagerly agreed. Unfortunately, the Canadian manufacturing partner they chose went out of business not long after, so things didn't get off to a great start. But the idea was solid, and they persevered. North South also attracted the attention of others, including Peter Mabeo, a furniture manufacturer from Botswana. "He had been watching what Jocelyn and I were doing." Peter thought Patty might have an understanding of the difficulties that manufacturers in the developing world face, and hired North South to work with him. "I was immediately struck by the similarities between these manufacturers and their respective communities."

Today, Patty has nothing but good things to say about her partners—that these remarkable people had the patience to put up with *her* for the years it took to figure out how to make North South a reality. "It was an investigation for both of us, with lots of learning and frustration, and not everyone would have endured that." Working with the craftspeople was another bonus. "The people who make these objects have an incredible level of skill that has been passed down through the generations. In addition, their work is very important to them personally, as part of their national identity. There is such humanity in every piece." It also made a world of difference to work with people who understand these artists and have access to their grassroots networks. "It's virtually impossible to walk into these places and get below the surface unless you've had an introduction of some sort."

The first North South products were launched at the International Contemporary Art Fair in New York, in May 2006, to huge acclaim. *Newsweek* named it one of their "Design Dozen," and

Metropolis gave it a great review. And North South is now working on new projects that combine twenty-first-century thinking with artisanal traditions. In Mexico, one of the state governments has funded a cluster of ceramics projects (tableware and tiles) and is determined to shift away from the mass production that characterized the past half century. In India, Patty is working with several companies that want to move out of handicrafts and into designed products, including furniture, textiles, and jewelry.

Patty confided that for many years she was obsessed with the idea that design is a frivolous field. It's clear that her view has changed: "Now I see that it can be much more than making one more thing that nobody needs. There's a real possibility to directly affect people's lives, to help them make a living, and to treasure the things they make—which are deeply and authentically imbued with meaning for these people." And that makes design a very satisfying thing, indeed.

MAKING A NAME FOR GOOD WORKS

Great moments in history—or in our own lives—can often be captured in a single image: one human being against a row of tanks in Tiananmen Square; a firefighter and flag atop the wreckage of the World Trade Center; the man on the moon. Or they can be summed up in a powerful phrase: "I have a dream," "Silent spring," or the line I've carried in my heart for several years: "A tiny ripple of hope." It comes from a speech Bobby Kennedy gave in 1966 to the National Union of South African Students' Day of Affirmation, in Cape Town, South Africa.

In September 2006, my good friend, Kerry Peacock, took me to the premiere of Emilio Estevez's movie about Robert F. Kennedy and the day of his assassination. *Bobby* is an extraordinarily moving portrait of this man and that year—1968—when the seeds of the New Radicals were sown. Through historical footage that appears throughout the film, I could feel Bobby's deep compassion and see his vision of peace and brotherhood. And I wasn't alone: people in the newsreel crowds reached out to touch him as he passed, because he gave voice to their deepest desires and to their hopes for the future. When the movie ended, every person inside Roy Thomson Hall rose to their feet in a roar and applauded the director and his all-star cast for five full minutes. This enthusiastic response was, in my view, a clear signal that, 40 years later, Bobby Kennedy's message is just as potent as ever. Perhaps more so. People want to be inspired, to feel hopeful about the world, and to lead meaningful lives.

I believe that we are poised on the verge of a new age—a positive, constructive, hopeful period in human history. And I know for certain that I am not alone in this view. For New Radicals-in-the-making like you, only one question remains: "Are you ready?"

Chapter 9

Are You Ready?

Fifty percent of the United States is currently experiencing unusually dry or drought conditions according to the U.S. Drought Monitor. The lack of water will be a rude awakening to American cities, especially in rapidly expanding areas such as the southwest. For instance, Los Angeles just had its driest year on record, and the mayor has asked residents to reduce water consumption. The population of California is expected to increase by 30 percent in the next twenty years.

—*Globe and Mail*, June 2007

Adrian Bradbury and Kieran Hayward heard about the "night commuters," the thousands of children who walk from rural areas to town centers in northern Uganda each night to avoid being abducted by a rebel paramilitary group. Immediately, they started GuluWalk to help draw attention to this issue and raise funds to help support these children.

It's not just the children of northern Uganda who are on the move. Adrian and Kieran are two among thousands, perhaps tens of thousands, of New Radicals who are walking their talk. As you can imagine, the stories in this book are just the tip of the iceberg. Sometimes, I close my eyes and think about all of the extraordinary men and women moving across this continent and around the world. By now, you will have noticed that there are connections between them. For instance, Liz Alderman, who lost her son in the World Trade Center attack, tells us: "At least we know what happened to our son. My heart goes out to the parents of the 30,000 children who have been kidnapped in northern Uganda. They don't have a clue where their children are, or even if they are alive." And now GuluWalk aims to help change that. Or how microlending flourished in one of the world's poorest countries, Bangladesh, and is now being employed to help the impoverished in the world's richest countries—including Canada's aboriginal people.

It's not the first time in history that so many people have wanted to do good. But it is the first time that "daily bread" and "good works" have come together for so many. My conversation with Zerofootprint's Ron Dembo came back to me as I sat down to write this chapter. He told me about "positive sum games"—a phrase economists use to describe situations in which everyone wins. Is there a better way to characterize this movement? We are creating roles that provide deep personal satisfaction *and* make a real difference in the lives of the less fortunate. As one client put it: "I'm beginning to appreciate just how privileged I am—that I can take the skills I have and use them to make a dent in the problems of the world. It doesn't get much better than that."

Some New Radicals were interested in talking about why so many people have come to the same conclusions at the same time. Mark Brayne, of the Dart Center, for example, said he is "somewhere between Carl Jung, one of the founders of psychoanalysis, and Richard Dawkins, the revolutionary evolutionist, on this." He believes that human consciousness reaches a certain point and then, just like any feature of any species, suddenly shifts into another gear. We talked about how every 20 years or so since World War II there has been such a shift. "Certainly 1968—I'm thinking of Vietnam and Paris—was one of those moments, and 1989—the fall of the Berlin Wall and Tiananmen Square—was another." We agreed that two things are influencing the current shift in consciousness: the Internet and our growing sense of connectedness, as well as our shared sense of vulnerability. I believe that global warming is a powerful catalyst—we understand that our individual actions are influencing a vast, complex ecosystem. It follows that what we do as individuals can also have a positive impact.

We are still in the early days of this movement. We don't know where it will take us, but I believe that the chances are pretty good that it will be in a positive, constructive, and hopeful direction. In fact, I sometimes picture a kind of global Möbius loop (a symbol of perpetuity): the more good we do, the more others benefit, which will lead to more goodwill and more good deeds, ad infinitum.

ARE YOU READY?

Only you can decide if this movement is for you, what your New Radical role will be, and how you'll get there. By reading this book, of course, you are no longer simply an observer. Even if you haven't taken the time to actually answer the first eight questions in detail, something in you has been stirred. I think of a rather impudent roadside sign I once came across when hopelessly lost in Scotland: "If you've come this far, you're well on your way!" The same applies to you, too. Of course, change can be difficult. It's hard to upset the status quo, even when we dearly want to move in a new direction, even when we know we'll reap huge rewards and drive social change.

Sometimes, at this stage my clients get cold feet. They find reasons to drop out. And many New Radicals I interviewed spoke candidly about the fear of failure rising up in them at a certain point. Even when they desperately wanted to change their lives—even when they felt that their psychic survival depended on it—some had real difficulty committing themselves. It's such a common human reaction. In academic circles, for instance, it's well known that Ph.D. candidates, well into their work, sometimes suddenly lose interest in it and find themselves unable to continue. As the English raconteur Augustus Hare wrote: "Half the failures of life arise from pulling one's horse as he is leaping." Suzanne Seggerman of Games for Change concurred. "We all have such a fear of failure," she said with a hint of sadness in her voice. "The other evening, I was reading my daughter a book about dinosaurs, and it really came home to me. 'We are just a little blip in time.' And I thought, 'What difference does it make if you fail? And if you succeed, your whole life will be so much better!'"

I can tell you that I was absolutely terrified that I would fail in the new role I was creating for myself. In fact, when I gave my first speech in Toronto, the fear factor was running so high in me that I fully expected to be ridiculed, or at least vigorously questioned, by a roomful of skeptics. In preparation, I crammed for a full week beforehand, and I even wrote a lighthearted defense into my remarks: "I recognize that some of you—or perhaps a nagging voice inside of each of us, nurtured on cynicism and despair at the enormity of the problems we face—may be thinking that my New Radicals idea is wildly optimistic, even a little mad. Which is why I'd like to leave you with this thought from George Bernard Shaw, who wrote: 'We want a few mad people now. See where the sane ones have landed us!'"

There may, of course, be good reasons for you to delay. You may have financial matters to attend to, such as waiting for a bonus to be paid, a pension to kick in, or an investment to mature. You may have financial obligations and responsibilities you can't ignore, such as a child who is still in school or a parent in a retirement home. There also may be personal matters to consider. For instance, many New Radicals told me that they wanted to take time to talk it over with their loved ones, knowing that those people also would be affected by the changes. Only you will know if it makes sense to wait—if the reasons that suddenly present themselves for the delay are valid and essential or simply a way to avoid the risk associated with reinventing what you do for a living.

But—I tell my clients—don't let these hesitations stop you altogether. Keep the spirit alive until you're ready to begin moving forward. Because, I say with deep compassion, we simply don't have time to sit on the fence any longer. If you're at midlife, as I am, you know that time is running out. And the same is true for our beloved Earth. By all means, do what you need to do, adjust your plan, put things in place, and, as Georgina Steinsky-Schwartz put it, "Look before you leap." But don't step off the path altogether.

MEETING NEW RADICALS AT THE TRAILHEAD

An extraordinary movement is waiting for you to take your place. I asked each New Radical I interviewed for this book to imagine sitting down with you over a cup of coffee—or a glass of wine. And then I asked them, "What would you say to this person who is considering becoming a New Radical?" As you can imagine, their responses covered a broad spectrum of ideas and emotions. Yet they also spoke with one voice, as if an opera chorus, using the Nike tagline that got this generation off the couch once before, "Just do it!" They hope, as I do, that their stories will awaken you to the power within and inspire you to take your place in the influential movement that is sweeping the world. Here, then, are 10 good reasons to become a New Radical:

1. **You will change someone's life.**

   "When I told the women in this village I would return in April, they were happy. I heard later that they didn't believe me, saying to one another, 'Why would she leave a rich and beautiful country to come and help strangers?' When I came back, there were tears. It was so important to me to return to Rwanda in April, you see, so that they knew something good could happen in that month."

   —Nicole Pageau, Ubuntu Edmonton

2. **You will change your own life.**
"I got an injection of energy and excitement about my ability to contribute to the world. It was incredibly scary to let go, but it was also incredibly freeing. And I have not been this happy in years."
—Melissa Dyrdahl, Bring Light

3. **Your skills are needed.**
"I can't think of any social cause that will say, 'That's it, we're done!' Everyone is toiling away at the things they care about. And there's always room for more people."
—Suzanne Seggerman, Games for Change

4. **You will discover the power of synchronicity.**
"I don't know how the universe works, and I'm not a scientist, but there's no doubt in my mind that there are a lot of synchronicities at work. The universe waits for you to say, 'I'm ready!' and when you've made the internal commitment, the universe, or whatever it is, just delivers. It's extraordinary. But, it takes that deep, courageous moment, or series of moments."
—Mark Brayne, Dart Center

5. **Your view of the world will change.**
"What I've learned from our alumni is the truly extraordinary impact they have on their kids' lives. It's funny, but it's fueled a sense of dissatisfaction at the same time. On the one hand, it's possible to achieve, and on the other, we still have so far to go to reach the point where all of our teachers attain that level of success with their children, and ultimately, where

the entire education system does, too. I've moved from having an idea that the world could be different, to realizing that not only should it, but that it really could."

—Wendy Kopp, Teach for America

6. **You will influence those around you.**

"This work has been a great example for my kids. My son, who is in university, is becoming interested in international affairs and is learning about the inequities between rich and poor countries. And he feels that social awareness has been in our family since he was a little boy, but now it's nice to be able to deliver on it, in terms of true on-the-ground activism. I can actually demonstrate how a bunch of people like me made a difference in this community."

—Tony Leighton, Guelph Civic League

7. **You will meet exceptional people.**

"A fascinating by-product that I didn't expect is that when you do this work, you start to meet really interesting people. I've developed a new network of friends. My personal life's gotten much better, and they are exactly the kind of people I want to develop this new venture with, as well."

—Ron Dembo, Zerofootprint

8. **You will feel connected to something bigger.**

"There are a lot of people out there who are disadvantaged and, you know, I could have been one. It's so important to help one another. I have friends who have all the material things in life, but aren't happy. I tell them they'll be amazed at what happens if they spend just one day a week helping someone in need."

—Paul Gillespie, Kids' Internet Safety Alliance (KINSA)

9. **You will play a part in saving the world.**

   "I've seen kids in refugee camps move from apathy and violence to happiness and hope for the future. They become children again."

   —Johann Koss, Right to Play

10. **You will die happy.**

    "I think the worst thing in the world is to be lying on your death bed saying, 'I wish I had tried.' Putting yourself out there, and giving yourself the opportunity to do some good, is noble in its own right. The other thing I tell people is that with the traditional career arc, the more money we make, the more we buy, and the more we make to keep feeding those things. In the process, we forget that we're not any happier, and maybe less so. To my mind, it's better to live 24 hours a day meaningfully rather than just the hours when you're not at work."

    —Kevin Salwen, *Motto* magazine

CREATING A NEW WORLD

As I was completing this book, the media were full of stories of the fortieth anniversary of the summer of love. It was a powerful reminder that millions of men and women who came of age under the influence of the '60s are turning their collective attention toward saving the world.

I have deep respect for my generation. There is a widespread misconception that—despite our idealistic beginnings—boomers haven't accomplished much. In some circles, we get credit only for becoming yuppies, driving SUVs, and inventing nonfat chai lattés. But, as Leonard Steinhorn points out in his thoughtful book, *The Greater Generation*, baby boomers have been responsible for a quiet revolution in social values: "Once the clamor of the sixties died down, boomers very quietly took the core values from that decade and began to remake society attitude by attitude . . . Empowered by their vast numbers and a network of like-minded peers, they became a generation unafraid to examine the precepts on which society and their identity stood."

If you think about the great social movements of our day—women's rights, gay and lesbian rights, minority rights, and human rights—boomers have played a major role. Yes, our parents—the Greatest Generation—introduced landmark civil rights laws, which helped pave the way for our work. But we were able to overturn decades, if not centuries, of norms, attitudes, and practices in a single generation. That's a lot to be proud of. And yet, as the research shows—and as New Radicals told me time and again—many of us believe our greatest contribution is yet to come. The youngest New Radical I interviewed (he's 29 years old), Sean Stannard-Stockton, director of tactical philanthropy for Ensemble Capital, summed it up nicely: "Bill Gates said that, at 52, he's got something more important to do than manage a software company. He wants to be remembered not as the guy who invented Microsoft, but as Gates the philanthropist. And I'll bet that most people can't remember what Rockefeller or Carnegie did professionally."

When I speak publicly about this movement, people always want to know when the tipping point will come. I used to struggle with the answer—who can predict the future? I'd talk about how hungry people are for this work, and how contagious this movement is. Then one day I realized that they were asking the wrong person. So now I simply hold up a mirror instead, so that they can see where the answer truly lies.

New Radical pioneers have been a beacon of light and hope. Their actions are a clarion call to the rest of us. What will your response be?

Bonus Chapter 1

Coda: More about the Movement

Nearly a third of Iraqis need emergency aid says Oxfam [the international organization that works with partners to find lasting solutions to poverty and injustice]. Eight million people are desperate for the necessities of life—food, water, shelter, medicine, and sanitation. Millions of others have fled the country. Many relief agencies have been unable to continue their work there, due to the war and widespread violence.

—Associated Press, July 2007

Musicians will know what *coda* means. As a word lover (and novice pianist), I had a pretty good idea of its definition. One morning, as I sat looking at the mountain of research I had not been able to incorporate in what I'd written so far, the word floated through my mind. I pulled out one of the massive dictionaries my father (also a writer) gave me and looked it up, just to be sure, and discovered that a coda is a passage at the end of a movement or composition, so as to form a more definitive and satisfactory conclusion. I laughed out loud. Was this a gentle suggestion from my dad, who died just as the new millennium—and New Radical age—was being born? In an instant, it seemed like the right thing to do, to add a new chapter that would offer more examples of the movement that is taking shape all around us. It would give me another chance to talk about the power of one—and to connect the dots between more New Radicals acts.

But how to tell the stories of these remarkable human beings? And which ones to include? Flipping through my files, I knew that I wanted to break bread with many of these extraordinary people, and I began to imagine a kind of gathering that would take place. I wanted to create a guest list that would embrace the widest possible range of good works, yet I knew that the result would be highly idiosyncratic. In truth, the real reason these New Radicals are invited to the party is because when I first heard about them, their work made me whoop with joy. They are positive, constructive, and hopeful people to the core.

As you wander through, you'll see more clearly what I've been saying at every opportunity: that New Radicals are appearing in every profession, every sector, and every place around the world. One day I'll have a snazzy slide show like Al Gore does—only mine will include a giant globe that I can schlep everywhere with me. It will light up to illustrate where New Radicals are at work. And a second set of lights will show the kinds of things that they are doing. At a glance, we will all be able to see just how widespread this movement is—and that we are all connected.

I've divided this coda into thirds (musicians may arch an eyebrow here): body, mind, and spirit. Each corresponds to the human experience and, roughly, to the divisions in our society and economy. Allow me to be your host, and guide you through from start to finish. Or, to continue the musical metaphor, feel free to sample this coda, dipping into sections that intrigue you.

Like any great gathering, I hope it fires your imagination, stirs your heart, and feeds your soul. Most of all, may it inspire you to think again and again: "I can do that!"

BODY

Food

Norman Borlaug is my first guest because he amply demonstrates the difference a single person can make. Norman, an agronomist whose work has saved the lives of a billion human beings, at the age of 93, is still going strong. In the middle of the last century, Norman developed hybrid dwarf wheat that tripled grain production in rural Mexico. Based on this success, the Rockefeller Foundation provided funding for him to bring agronomists from around the world to learn his planting and soil conservation techniques. By 1965, he had helped India and Pakistan introduce high-yield agricultural methods and increase their output sevenfold. In the mid-1970s, he was behind similar advances in China. How has this changed our world? In 1960, 60 percent of the world went hungry each day. By 2000, just 14 percent did. But Norman knows that this means some 850,000 men, women, and children still don't have enough to eat. And that is why this New Radical Innovator continues his work. Today, the Bill and Melinda Gates Foundation is helping him make a difference in Africa, where famine is a constant threat.

Another invited guest is Cary Fowler, an American who is creating the ultimate icebox for seeds. Cary is executive director of the Global Crop Diversity Trust. The trust's job is to collect 3 million domestic and wild seeds from around the world and store them in a place that will withstand catastrophe: safeguarding the world's food supply against nuclear war, climate change, terrorism, rising sea levels, and the collapse of energy systems. "If worst came to worst, we could reconstruct agriculture on this planet." Where is this $3 million refrigerator that some people are calling a modern-day Noah's Ark? The Norwegian government built the Svalbard International Seed Vault deep inside a sandstone mountain lined with permafrost on the Norwegian Arctic island of Spitsbergen, about 600 miles (966 kilometers) from the North Pole. The vault has reinforced concrete walls more than 3-feet (1-meter) thick, two air locks, and high-security blast-proof doors. But the best protection for the world's most famous food store? "The mountains are patrolled by polar bears."

Other New Radicals are hard at work protecting not just the seeds farmers sow, but their very way of life. Countries that barely contribute to global warming are scrambling to survive dramatic and rapid changes to their climate, and farmers are on the front lines. Through an organization called Practical Action, people like Gehendra Gurung are helping growers adapt to changing conditions and prepare for what's to come. Gehendra is working in Nepal, helping farmers build dikes; set up early-warning systems for floods; and learn how to grow crops that work in the new climate, store water and irrigate, control new pests, introduce renewable energy, and encourage reforestation. "Every part of their world is changing. For instance, on the north side of the Himalayas, normally in the rain shadow of the monsoons, there is much more rain, and people are discovering that flat mud roofs don't keep it out. So they are adding pitched roofs to their buildings." And Practical Action is making a difference, villagers say. Against his father's advice, Davandrod Kardigarch, a young Nepalese farmer, switched from cereal crops, which need water at precise times of year, to bananas and vegetables. Now that he's seeing results, even Dad has come onside.

Of course, farmers in developing countries aren't the only ones who need to learn new ways of being in the world. As the Sierra Club's Martin LeBlanc noted in Chapter 5, several generations have come of age with only a tangential connection to nature. Baby boomers will remember Frances Moore Lappé's 1970s bestseller, *Diet for a Small Planet*, which said we could address world hunger by becoming vegetarians (a radical idea at the time). Now her daughter, Anna, and partner Bryant Terry are introducing a new generation to the delights and advantages of eating sustainably. And they're doing it by making it all cool: they are holding what they call Grub Parties, where people can gather to talk about—and enjoy—food that is grown with respect for the environment and for growers and that isn't picked before it's ripe and shipped halfway across the world. Notes Anna: "You know that old truism, 'You are what you eat'? Grub is all about turning that idea around. In fact, I am what *you* eat. Everything works in systems, and all our choices are connected."

Environment

Retired Navy Vice Admiral Conrad C. Lautenbacher, Jr. is coming to the party, because he's the American cochairman of an astonishing international project. GEONETCast brings information about the state of the planet together in a single source. Thousands of smaller systems that keep tabs on things like agriculture and forests, water and air quality, weather and ocean currents, can now feed this information to GEO satellites. And governments and other organizations will be able to make use of this unprecedented one-stop resource beginning in 2008. "GEONETCast will help us take the pulse of the planet. It integrates, for instance, environmental data with data about disease vectors, pollutants, rainfall, and sea surface temperatures, so that we can predict, mitigate, and maybe even prevent health threats before they become crises." Australians will be able to keep a close watch on drought conditions; Brazilians, their forests; Canadians, their changing Arctic. Mozambique will be able to forecast outbreaks of insect-borne diseases such as malaria. Governments around the world will have serious help in reducing the loss of life and property during and after disasters, may be able to improve weather forecasting, and will find new ways to manage resources. There are commercial applications, too. For instance, insurance companies can keep closer track of what's going on around the world, so as to better understand risks.

Many people believe that water will soon surpass oil as the world's most precious resource. At the moment, who will be water-rich seems a bit like a game of musical chairs. As I wrote this chapter, Britain had just suffered one of its wettest summers ever, much of the American Midwest was under water, and 200 million people had been left homeless by monsoons in Southeast Asia. In contrast, 50 percent of Greece was on fire, and parts of Australia, Africa, Canada, China, and India were experiencing drought conditions.

In Chapter 1, I used the water-in-a-box story as a prime example of the New Radical trend I saw emerging. It turns out that the man behind this invention, Dennis McGuire, holds some 400 patents, and innovative clean air and water technologies are his new passion. Ecosphere Technologies' portable water system uses wind and solar to purify H_2O, and it also generates power. Fold out its solar panels, and they can provide enough electricity for half a dozen homes and power for the wireless satellite link that comes with the system—so that aid workers and residents can surf the Internet and make phone calls up to 31 miles (50 kilometers) away. In March 2007, Dennis demonstrated his company's mobile water purification system to the U.S. Federal Emergency Management Agency (FEMA). This time, it's water-in-a-box-on-a-truck. The system can move quickly into devastated areas and provide up to 72,000 gallons (272,550 liters) of clean water per day.

Fire is the element that fascinates another New Radical Entrepreneur. Hindu funeral pyres contribute more than seven and a half million tons (seven million tonnes) of carbon dioxide to the atmosphere each year, and consume 50 million trees in the process. Others have tried to design alternatives, but they have met with resistance from traditionalists. Until now. The Indian nonprofit organization Mokshda Paryavaran Evam Van Suraksha Samiti (Mokshda PEVSS) offers an open-air platform with a roof and chimney that controls temperature and air circulation. Overall burning time is reduced from six hours to two, and the fuel required drops from a little over 1,100 pounds (500 kilograms) to just 220 pounds (100 kilograms), Mokshda PEVSS's Anshul Garg said. "People are very sentimental and emotional about these issues. To make it acceptable to traditionalists is a huge accomplishment." The company hopes to further improve its efficiency and to close the loop: ashes would be used to fertilize plantations of trees grown to feed the pyres.

Waste is another pressing issue for human societies: landfills are messy, smelly, toxic wastes of space that no one wants in his or her backyard. Incinerating garbage is highly efficient, but also extremely expensive and equally unpopular. And now a University of Calgary environmental engineering professor has developed a third option. New Radical Innovator Patrick Hettiaratchi's idea is based on bio-cells. Each clay and plastic-lined cell is loaded with more than 55,000 tons (50,000 tonnes) of garbage (anything and everything can go in) and capped with a membrane that lets water in but keeps odor from escaping. Oxygen is forced out, water is added, and leachate (the liquid that forms as the trash decays) is filtered through to hasten decomposition. Over the three to five years that it takes to decompose, enough methane gas can be captured to produce 300 kilowatt-hours of power. Then, when it's cooked, the compost is removed, the recyclables reclaimed, and the residue goes to landfill. "We've got some test cells in place now and are looking at how to adapt the technology to other regions of the world. In a humid country, for instance, it would decompose much faster."

As resources grow more scarce, more than just garbage will be mined. In Ghana, New Radical Entrepreneur Wayne Dunn has found what he believes is buried treasure. Four decades ago, when Ghana dammed the Black and White Volga rivers to create a source of hydroelectric power, entire forests were submerged in the process. These trees remain rooted to the bottom of the lake the dam created, Lake Volta, and are a constant danger to boaters—ferries and fishers alike. Wayne and his company, Clark Sustainable Resource Developments Ltd., have been given permission to harvest the mahogany, ebony, and other hardwoods that are under the lake. It's a midlife turnaround for Wayne, who dropped out of high school to become a logger and then went back to school to earn his MBA. He was inspired by a television program about the lake and its trees.

"We believe it's the largest and most valuable source of underwater timber in the world." And he's hired a consultant from the Nature Conservancy to ensure that the venture also provides social and environmental returns. For instance, the lake's endangered West African manatees—trapped since the dam was built, and no longer able to migrate to the ocean—will be protected.

Health

Demographers project that, by 2050, one person in five will be a senior citizen. People in the west often hear about the aging population—whether the pension and health systems will support senior citizens and what must be redesigned to accommodate the aging boomer generation—but westerners are not the only people on the planet who are getting on in years. There are more than 100 million older people around the world today. And the problems of senior citizens in the west pale in comparison to some of those in developing countries where millions of men and women live on less than a dollar a day.

HelpAge International is a global network of nonprofit organizations working with disadvantaged older people around the globe, particularly in developing countries. The group's work in Darfur illustrates well what it does. The United Nations estimates that 300,000 people have died from disease and malnutrition in that country since fighting began in 2003. Millions more in Darfur are homeless, and of these, perhaps 10 percent are old. Life under such conditions is difficult when a person is young and able-bodied. Just imagine what it must be like when it is difficult to walk, much less reach food registration points and health treatment centers. HelpAge's Mathew Cherian and his teams are working in camps in western Darfur where there are high concentrations of older people (who often look after orphans as well as themselves). Mathew says that, "We're establishing older people's committees to act as their voice with aid agencies and to help them find ways to work together to support one another. For instance, they are talking about how to reduce their isolation, finding ways to earn a little money, and growing food in gardens on the camp perimeters. But we're also lobbying at the highest levels so that the needs of the elderly are understood."

In some parts of the world, getting the medicines people need into their hands is a huge problem. This is particularly true in places where transportation systems do not exist or are unreliable, as in many parts of the vast African continent. One health-care worker can be responsible for up to 20,000 people spread over many miles of harsh terrain—and many men, women, and children die each day simply because they cannot be reached.

Riders for Health is changing all that. It's a nonprofit organization that has established a system of two- and four-wheeled vehicles to take medical personnel and supplies where they are needed. Today, Riders for Health is providing three countries—Gambia, Zimbabwe, and Nigeria—with this health-care delivery system, and the group intends to keep growing. Riders for Health is the brainchild of transplanted Brits Barry and Andrea Coleman. Andrea is a former motorcycle racer and operations director for Team Castrol-Herron, and Barry is a journalist who has written for the *Guardian*, BBC, and *Forbes* magazine. Together, they have decided to put their knowledge of the motorcycling community to good use. And they keep introducing new innovations. For example, in Africa, where 1 in 14 women dies in childbirth (compared to 1 in 5,000 in the developed world), Riders has introduced the Uhuru, a specially designed motorcycle sidecar for women in life-threatening labor.

Moving east, we come to Sonika Verma, a doctor at India's Council of Scientific and Industrial Research, who is working on cutting-edge diabetic research with a New Radical twist. One thousand-year-old manuscripts from India's three major ancient systems of medicine are her resource. In fact, Dr. Verma switched from practicing traditional medicine to study them, and she has been joined by hundreds of colleagues. This exciting development has huge implications for the country. The manuscripts will certainly yield information that is useful to Indian physicians. It will also help create remedies for the poor. As the World Bank's John Lambert pointed out: "Many people in developing countries cannot afford to buy aspirin." And the boost in demand for these remedies will increase the earning power of those who collect medicinal plants for a living.

But there is another benefit that has global implications. Dr. Verma and her colleagues are creating a database that will help protect India against biopiracy. That database—in five languages—will be accessible by patent offices worldwide. Other countries with traditional systems of medicine they want to protect—for example, Sri Lanka, Pakistan, and Cambodia—are watching India's lead closely. The bigger challenge will come when countries with strong oral traditions—such as those in Africa—struggle to find ways to collect, store, and monetize their knowledge.

Another woman has found a very different way of improving the health of India's poorest. Jessica Kerwin had a life many people aspire to—she was a fashion journalist based in Paris—when she had a wake-up call: her marriage came apart at the seams. She responded by quitting her job, moving to India, and becoming a masseuse for people with leprosy. She spends her days soothing old women with missing digits, withered limbs, and broken noses. "Many of these women, some well into their seventies, have barely been touched, except to be bandaged, for decades." Jessica had chosen carefully—she works at Anandwan, a community founded by the Hindu lawyer, Baba Amte (a contemporary of Gandhi), who has devoted his life to helping the country's so-called untouchables. Jessica said that Amte, at the age of 92, is considered a living saint. I will say, when I introduce you to her, that I consider her to be one, too.

MIND

Energy

A Dutch company has discovered that you can generate electricity by mixing freshwater and saltwater, and it says that "blue power" plants can be created anywhere that rivers run into the sea. Cees Buisman, director of research and development at Wetsus, an innovative water-technology institute, and professor of biological recycling technology at Wageningen University, said: "In a country like the Netherlands, 3,300 cubic meters [871,767 gallons] of freshwater run into the ocean every second. Taken together, you could generate enough electricity to supply 25 percent of Dutch households."

He's talking about reverse electrodialysis (RED), which works like this: when freshwater and saltwater meet, the level of salt falls (the freshwater dilutes the saltwater). During the process, energy is created, and that energy can be captured. Brilliantly simple, isn't it? Wetsus researchers are planning to install membrane filters on the Afsluitdijk dam in northern Holland. "If it works, you could close down all the nuclear and coal stations in the northern provinces." And he sees opportunities worldwide: "Look at a map of the world. Lots of cities are located on the ocean. These are precisely the places where we can generate blue power."

German scientists Dr. Gerhard Knies and Dr. Franz Trieb have their eye on another untapped source of energy. They want to harness the desert sun, saying that covering just 0.5 percent of the world's hot deserts with concentrating solar power (CSP) could provide for the entire world's energy needs. CSP uses mirrors to concentrate the sun's rays on a pipe or vessel filled with gas or liquid. As the pipes heat up, they power conventional steam turbines. The technology also produces desalinated water as a byproduct, which can be used for drinking and air-conditioning.

In San Diego, California, a New Radical inventor noticed that people sometimes objected to wind farms cluttering up the view, and he began to imagine a sky-based system. Sky WindPower's Dave Shepard started his career in World War II cracking Japanese military codes and went on to develop machines that read written text. His new company's flying generator has been described as a cross between a helicopter and a kite. An H-shaped frame is tethered to the ground by a long cable. Four routers provide the lift needed to keep it aloft and turn dynamos that generate electricity. Ken Caldeira, the climate scientist at the Carnegie Institution (see Chapter 3), has worked with Dave and says that, "Harvesting just 1 percent of the energy of the jet stream would produce enough power for the entire planet."

And a fourth New Radical idea connects these new sources of energy together. Jürgen Schmid, head of the alternative-energy Institute für Solare Energieversorgungtechnik (Institute of Solar Energy Technology, ISET) at Germany's University of Kassel, says that the problem with renewables is that the sun isn't always shining, or it may be shining in the Sahara when cloudy Ireland needs power. But ultra-high-voltage transmission lines could deliver this energy wherever and whenever it's needed. Why isn't this being done now? Current energy distribution grids are alternating current (AC), and they lose much of their power over long distances. In contrast, direct current (DC) is a far more efficient way to transmit electricity between distant points. Jürgen envisages an international DC grid that could supply much of the world's energy needs from renewable sources: blue power, desert sun, wind power, whatever the case may be. The Global Energy Network Institute in California agrees wholeheartedly. It sees a future where DC lines could be used to bring Americans solar energy from the Sahara and wind and geothermal power from South America and Siberia.

The mind reels.

At the same time, New Radicals are busy designing products that will help lessen our "footprint." Plastic bags have come under intense scrutiny and are the source of some pretty creative thinking. This is, shall we say, corn's moment in the sun, not only as a new fuel source, but as biodegradable packaging and bags. NatureWorks, the largest lactic-acid plant in the world, is producing a resin known as polylactic acid (PLA). This resource, being manufactured on the shores of the Missouri River in Nebraska (the heart of America's farm country), has several things going for it. It's renewable—as opposed to conventional plastic bags, which consume about 200,000 barrels of oil a day in the United States alone. And it's compostable—it breaks down, even in landfills. NatureWorks' CEO Dennis McGrew said that, in the United States, "Newman's Own Organics, Wild Oats, and Wal-Mart are using PLA products." One wonders if "plastic" bags will soon appear only in museums, as many municipalities around the world are outlawing them altogether.

Speaking of trash, soon you can forget throwing all that paper from your photocopier away—or even into the recycling bin. Xerox researchers tell me that they are working on an erasable paper that would allow you to reuse it until it falls apart. At the company's fabled Palo Alto Research Center, the team discovered that 44.5 percent of the 1,200 pages an average office worker prints are for daily use. That is, they are read and discarded in a single shift. Brinda Dlala, an anthropologist at the center, says that their prototype system produces documents where printed information disappears within 16 hours and that the paper can be reused up to 50 times.

Can retailers be New Radicals, too? Ian Yolles thinks so. He's vice president of brand communication for Nau, an outdoor clothing company. Nau (Maori for welcome, and pronounced "now") stands out from the competition in three important ways. First, to save money and energy Nau has introduced Webfronts—small stores where you can shop and take your purchases home with you or opt to have them shipped for free from Nau's warehouse. Better yet, if you choose delivery, you get 10 percent off. What you buy is different, too. The company's gear is made from the most eco-advanced fabrics and is wonderfully fashionable (which is a real boon for hikers like me who have grown weary of baggy blue pants). Plus, every transaction becomes a charitable donation: 5 percent goes to a cause of your choosing. By 2010, if the company meets its goals, it will be giving away $13 million a year. Nau has been open for only a few months, but it is already attracting plenty of attention: the August 2007 issue of *Time* magazine has named them as one of 25 creative visionaries.

And what about the $100 laptop? You have undoubtedly heard about the One Laptop Per Child (OLPC) Initiative, which was cofounded by Nicholas Negroponte who also was director of the MIT Media Laboratory. The company intends to supply children in the developing world with simple, easy to use, low-power computers. The laptops recently moved from wild idea to workable prototype. Mary Lou Jepsen, OPLC's chief technologist, found a way to modify the display and cut screen costs. She also reduced power consumption by 80 percent. And now, Negroponte has announced, they are ready to launch. Users of XO, the rugged little green laptop, can choose between a battery, solar power, a tiny windmill, or a hand or foot crank. The first batch goes to the world's poorest kids in 2007, at a cost of $176 each (as production goes up, costs will go down). You may be thinking, as I was when I heard this news, "I want one!" You'll soon have your chance. In 2008, the group will launch a "buy two, get one" campaign, so that one laptop goes to a child in need and one comes home with you.

Staying in gift-giving mode, the good people at Changing the Present are doing just that: they have come up with a way for people to give meaningful gifts. Their Web site offers a fascinating collection of causes—everything from wheelchairs for landmine victims to ways to help pay for eye surgery, protect one acre of the rain forest, or sponsor an hour of cancer research. President Robert Tolmach told me: "Just imagine what we could do with just a fraction of the $250 billion Americans spend each year on gifts."

Social Entrepreneurship

The application of management skills to the achievement of social ends is what social entrepreneurs are all about. Peter Drucker summed up this trend in typically succinct fashion: social entrepreneurs raise the "performance capacity of society." There are thousands of such entrepreneurs in place now, and more appear each day. Here are two I'd like you to meet.

There is a growing conflict between human societies and wild animals, as we encroach on their territories or carve those areas up with highways and shipping lanes. In Africa, for instance, villagers have had great difficulty keeping elephants out of their crops. They have, that is, until zoologist Loki Osborn devised a plan that stopped the snacking pachyderms in their tracks. Each field is now surrounded by a thin rope coated with a paste made from hot chilies. Because elephants have supersensitive trunks, they avoid coming into contact with the spicy strings. And the chili peppers are more than a way to keep elephants, buffalo, and other animals out of fields—they have become a cash crop. The chilies are being made into bottled hot sauces, jams, and relishes. "They're grown as buffer crops to prevent raiding and are harvested and sold on the world market through the Elephant Pepper [Development] Trust."

Business school grad Farouk Jiwa runs East Africa's largest honey production company, Honey Care Africa, which has increased the income of 9,000 small Kenyan farm households by 50 percent. Farouk distributes wooden beehives to farmers, and the beekeepers sell their honey back to him at fair trade prices. In addition to helping farmers increase their standard of living, the bees help to maintain vegetation diversity (through pollination) and reduce deforestation (farmers don't need to sell firewood to supplement their income). Interestingly, bees have the same effect upon elephants as do chilies: the animals are more afraid of bees than humans, and they tend to stay away from those crops being pollinated by the bees. Given the mysterious problem plaguing bees in North America and Europe—known as colony collapse disorder—Farouk is onto a good thing. Soon, African beekeepers may be exporting their honey (and perhaps bees?) around the world.

Finance

Honey Care Africa, Elephant Pepper Development Trust, and other social entrepreneurs need both seed money and ongoing sources of capital. Some of them call on established agencies. For example, Honey Care Africa, was launched with a loan from the Danish government's International Development Agency. Others are turning to new organizations that have embraced the ancient practice of microloans. Also known as microfinance and micro-credit, this practice entered the consciousness of New Radicals thanks to the efforts of Muhammad Yunus and his Grameen Bank. In reality, it has long been in practice in countries such as Ghana, India, Mexico, Sri Lanka, and Bolivia.

The practice turns out not to be new to North America, either. For 20 years a nonprofit bank has been quietly doing business in San Francisco, and it now boasts $90 million in repaid loans, $100 million in current investments, and $50 million on loan. Mark Finser and his RSF Social Finance Bank were ahead of the curve.

There's another innovator financier that I'd like you to meet. Robert Chambers had a successful career as an electrical engineer, and he even did a stint in the U.S. Navy. Reluctant to retire, he agreed to help a friend in the car business. What he discovered—salespeople pressuring poor folks into buying expensive cars with high interest rates—appalled him. So he created Bonnie CLAC (Car Loans and Counseling) in response. "A car is a necessity to get and keep a job, especially in rural areas where there's little or no transportation." Robert's organization helps people buy new base-model cars at prices he's negotiated with dealers. And, thanks to Robert's organization, purchasers buy them with loans from local banks with terms usually offered only to those with good credit.

Kiva.org uses the power of the Internet to connect lenders with small-business owners in developing countries. Its site lists hundreds of projects at any given time, and it has helped 70,000 people lend money to 11,000 entrepreneurs. Founder Matt Flannery, a former programmer at TiVo, and his wife, Jessica, spent time working in rural Kenya, Tanzania, and Uganda, and they were struck by the power small business has to change people's futures. They have started their Web-based organization as a way to help people like you and me help the less fortunate help themselves.

With microlending well established, I was delighted to discover there is a new way to help the world's poor find financial peace of mind. Opportunity International Micro Insurance Agency is the world's first insurance broker for the poor. It designs, distributes, and administers insurance for individual clients, as well as works with organizations such as World Vision and Habitat for Humanity. With monthly premiums as low as $1 a month for a family of five, insurance is now available to those most at risk. President and CEO Christopher Crane cites the AIDS crisis in Africa as an example: "With no insurance coverage, funeral costs can decimate personal savings and assets." Opportunity International is also pioneering other innovative insurance products. Working with the World Bank in Malawi, for instance, it has introduced weather-indexed crop insurance, alleviating the high risk of drought and its impact on crop yields.

The tax system is also being used to drive change, with London's mayor Ken Livingstone as an inspirational case in point. In an effort to reduce traffic and pollution in central London, the mayor introduced a congestion tax of five British pounds (£5, a little more than US$10) per vehicle in central London—with proceeds earmarked for public transit. Though this New Radical Innovator was widely criticized at first, his wild idea has been a huge success: congestion has been reduced by 20 percent, and levels are expected to drop by an additional 15 percent now that the tax has been raised to eight pounds (£8, about US$16.50). Londoners, tourists, and business owners are grateful for improvements in inner-city life, and the idea is catching on. Other parts of London will introduce it, as will other cities across Europe (and, one hopes, other parts of the world).

Everything in our world seems to revolve around money. And, for most of us, this reality is accompanied by a constant shortage of the stuff. Bernard Lietaer, formerly an economist and banker (he was one of the people behind Europe's common currency), and now a professor and author, believes there is an alternative. He's proposing that a complementary money system be introduced alongside the existing one. Based on barter, it would allow transactions when "money" isn't available. It's not such a wild idea (though a distinctly New Radical one); Lietaer likens it to frequent-flier miles, which is something we are all familiar with. "It's all about cooperation—systems that support the community, that make things possible. Imagine a world where you could cash in your talents even if there were no official market for them." It's an idea that seems to be catching on: in 1990 there were 100 known complementary money systems in the world, today there are more than 4,000. His Access Foundation is an alliance of such systems, and it provides information for people wanting to get one started.

Building

So many people are doing good in the area of architecture and construction, and I've invited three who are doing New Radical work.

Quietly working away in South Africa where his wife is posted with the United Nations, French architect Eric Bigot has dreamed up ZenKaya. His company creates simple, sustainable prefabricated housing: manufactured mobile homes that he believes will bring homeownership within reach of ordinary South Africans. He also hopes that construction of the homes will help stimulate the economy. "South Africa is crippled by an unemployment rate of 25 percent." One wonders if there's an organization that could offer micromortgages to hopeful home buyers.

Architect Tye Farrow brought elements of nature—sunlight, living trees, and natural materials—into the design of Toronto's Credit Valley Hospital to help create a feeling of ease and relaxation, and to bring symbols of life into a place concerned with illness and death. The International Academy for Design and Health took note and honored him with its first Architect Award, in recognition of his "contribution to health and humanity through the medium of architecture and design." And, importantly in these cost-conscious times, he did it all under budget. It's clear that this effort was much more than just another billable project for this New Radical. "We are here to do something, to participate as citizens. We each have a role to transform what's in front of us and make it better."

Travis Price is an environmental pioneer credited with coining the term "passive solar." He is now leading the development of sustainable architecture—building homes and public spaces that take not just the physical environment into account but also the spirit of a place. "My idea of sustainability is that it honors both nature and culture. We need to be asking about more than our environmental resources. We also need to know about our mythical, cultural, metaphorical responses to the land." Travis teaches a course in Spirit of Place/Spirit of Design at The Catholic University of America's School of Architecture and Planning. He's on the invitation list because he's introducing us to new ways of thinking about our living and working environments.

Travel

Tourism is definitely an industry in transition, as concerns about global warming—and other travel-related environmental issues—increase. All kinds of options are in place (carbon offsetting—a way to counterbalance the environmental impact of our actions, specifically the creation of CO_2, through other activities that reduce carbon levels, such as the planting of trees—for example), while others are coming—including, in 2008, the end of the paper ticket era for airlines, which the International Air Transport Association says will save about 50,000 trees a year.

And what of the aircraft? Aviation engineers are hard at work on planes that will use less fuel. One group is focusing its attention on something that has dropped off the radar screen in recent years. The Silent Aircraft Initiative has a bold aim: to design an airplane where noise reduction is a major consideration. "So quiet that its noise would be imperceptible outside an urban airport in the daytime," was how Ann Dowling of Cambridge University described it. It surprised me to learn that the basic design of commercial aircraft hasn't changed in more than half a century. The team's alternative concept aircraft—the SAX-40—blends fuselage and wing.

Because it's more aerodynamic and produces less turbulence, it also makes less noise. Zoltan Spakovsky of the Massachusetts Institute of Technology (MIT) added that "the integral system design, not one particular technology, enables the low noise." These New Radical Innovators will be joined by commercial partners including Boeing, Rolls-Royce, and British Airways.

Some New Radicals are even inventing alternatives to travel. Author Margaret Atwood has fans on five continents but, after 30 years on the road, was growing rather tired of book signing trips: "As I whizzed around on yet another tour, getting up at four in the morning to catch a plane, doing two cities in one day, and eating out of the mini-bar at the end of the day because I was too tired to call room service, I wondered if there wasn't a better way." She's invented the LongPen, a device that allows her to meet fans all over the world—and to sign their books—from the comfort of her own home. Here's how it works: An Internet video chat is set up between a bookstore and Atwood's home. A fan sits at a desk in, say, Melbourne, Australia, and speaks for a few moments with Margaret. The author then writes a message on a touchpad on her desk, which the LongPen reproduces in the book held in the reader's hands. "You don't have to be in the same room as someone to have a meaningful exchange." A sign of things to come, perhaps?

There's one more travel-related guest. On his trip to hilly Rwanda, Tom Ritchey noticed how the coffee crop was being shipped to market: on the back of rickety bicycles. Not only was this method for getting the beans to market exhausting for the hard-working farmers, but the coffee was often not at its best when it arrived at the market, and a lower-grade bean meant less money for growers overall. Happily, Tom, one of the inventors of the mountain bike, immediately began to draw up plans for a two-wheeled, heavy-duty cargo bike with an extended storage area at the rear that can carry up to 300 pounds (136 kilograms). He's launching his pilot project in Rwanda, where he intends to build a factory to manufacture the bikes.

Communication

After 12 years as an anchor at the American cable news network CNN, Daryn Kagan has had intimate knowledge of the terrible stories that have taken place around the planet. She was in the anchor seat, for instance, on September 11, 2001. Not long ago, she realized that she really wanted to spend her time talking about good news, and so she launched a Web site "dedicated to the radical idea that the world is a good place." DarynKagan.com features a daily Webcast of stories that "show the world what's possible," and it has become a regular destination for people looking for stories to inspire their day. Daryn's on my list.

SPIRIT

Religion

A good place to begin is with Kevin Dowling, the Roman Catholic bishop of the diocese of Rustenberg in South Africa, who has set up a small clinic to advise people how to protect themselves from HIV. How? "They must use condoms." That puts him in the opposite corner from Rome, which forbids the use of condoms under any circumstances. In southern Africa, Dowling is known as the "AIDS bishop." There are many who admire him, and even some who do as he does, if a little more quietly. The Vatican is preparing a statement on the use of condoms by people with HIV (though its current position is that abstinence is the only option), which people like the AIDS bishop hope will be a major change of policy.

In Britain, meanwhile, the Church of England is going green. It is conducting an environmental audit of all places of worship and administration, in an effort to dramatically "reduce their footprint" by 2008. And the Bishop of London, Richard Chartres, most delightfully, has suggested that unnecessary air travel or Hummer ownership may become the new sin. (This last point is not terribly positive, constructive, or hopeful, but what's a good sermon without a little guilt?)

In Buddhist circles, leaders such as Thich Nhat Hanh are waving the banner of engaged Buddhism—that is, encouraging practitioners to get off their comfortable, even complacent, cushions and out into the community. In Redwood City, California, for instance, the Sati Center is offering training for Buddhist practitioners who want to respond more directly to the suffering of the world. Gil Frondsal, a Zen priest, describes it as the kind of one-on-one service traditionally associated with chaplains: "that is, people who offer spiritual care in hospitals, hospices, schools, and prisons."

One profoundly New Radical idea that I've been watching for several years is the Network of Spiritual Progressives. Rabbi Michael Lerner, one of its founders, is definitely on the list. This grassroots interfaith organization sees itself as a consciousness-raising movement. Its work is based on two core ideas: a New

Bottom Line and a Spiritual Covenant with America. "We want to reshape the economic, political, and social life in accordance with a New Bottom Line of loving, caring, generosity, kindness, ethical and ecological sensitivity, and awe and wonder at the grandeur of creation." The covenant (which echoes Newt Gingrich's Contract with America) establishes a policy platform for critical areas such as education, health, and the environment. The health part of the covenant, for instance, recognizes that "human beings are not just physical beings, but also psychological and spiritual beings—and we need health care that deals with the whole." The Spiritual Progressive's latest idea is a Global Marshall Plan, which aims to reestablish trust and hope among the peoples of the world so that we might begin to act cooperatively on the issues that face us. The question that informs the plan is this: "What serves all the people on this planet and best serves the survival of the planet itself?"

Culture and Cultural Renewal

Literacy lies at the heart of every civilization, and numerous New Radicals have taken up a new role as advocates for a literacy initiative. Here are two very different examples of men who are staking their lives—and their livelihoods—on libraries.

Twenty percent of Brazilians are illiterate, and 60 percent are functionally illiterate (that is, they cannot read a newspaper or write a letter). The Brazilian government is working closely with local nongovernmental organizations to increase literacy across the nation, and one New Radical is doing his bit. Carlos Leite had been a handyman for more than three decades, when one day he came upon three abandoned encyclopedias, and he was immediately seized by the idea of setting up a library. Fifty-one years old and functionally illiterate, he is now the librarian of Jardim Catarina, a shantytown of about 100,000 people, some 31 miles (50 kilometers) from Rio de Janeiro. The shack that was once his home now houses a collection 6,000 strong. He feels that he's found his life's work: "I was brought up here, I know what this place needs. Today, even if I wanted to close this library, I couldn't. It belongs to the people now."

Each day brings more news about Baghdad, a city under siege. Many have died, others have fled, and millions are struggling to survive. Saad Eskander has bravely waded into this mêlée with a clear mission: to save the national library. Once home to ancient works of Arab literature, as well as to a vast archive of Ottoman, British, and Ba'ath material, the library was looted and burned during the earliest days of the war. Saad estimates that 60 percent of its collection was stolen or destroyed, including most of its rare books. A Kurdish historian who lived in exile for many years (and studied at the London School of Economics), Saad sees rebuilding it as a way to help create a better future for Iraqis. It is an unbelievably complicated, difficult, and dangerous task that ranges from buying books discovered in street markets to asking for microfilm copies of official documents stored in London, all while he faces death threats and terrorist attacks of the building, not to mention the difficulty of getting to work each day in a city full of roadblocks and military checkpoints. Why does he do it? "The same reason Iraqi children go to school each day. If the library closes, we have nothing to bind us together."

The same region so stirred the heart of Rory Stewart, a member of Britain's Foreign Office, that he spent several years walking across Pakistan, Iran, Afghanistan, India, and Nepal—a journey of some 6,000 miles (9,656 kilometers). Today, Rory lives in Kabul, Afghanistan, where he is chief executive of the Turquoise Mountain Foundation, created by the Prince of Wales and Afghanistan President Hamid Karzai. The foundation works to preserve Afghanistan's rich architectural and cultural heritage, which has had to survive not only war but also the pressures of modern-day development. Among other programs, Turquoise Mountain is training men and women in traditional woodwork, calligraphy, and ceramics. It is also working to rebuild and regenerate the historic commercial center of Kabul, including saving historic buildings and constructing a new bazaar as well as galleries for traditional craft businesses. "It's not simply about architecture or heritage. What is at stake is the dignity of human beings."

Human Rights

In Uganda, a former policewoman has started a women's shelter. While that may sound ordinary to us, in Africa it is revolutionary. Hellen Alyek has created a safe haven in a nondescript hut on the outskirts of Lira, a town on the edge of Uganda's troubled northern region. (It's where the Aldermans first started their work to alleviate the suffering of people in postconflict countries, as described in Chapter 2, and where GuluWalk helps to protect children.) Like western shelters, the one in Lira keeps a low profile. Inside, though, secrets are shared: stories about broken bones, sex attacks, and horrors too awful to contemplate. Twelve-year-old Grace, for instance, was collecting firewood near her village when a passing soldier raped her. Soon, she will deliver her baby in the safety of this new community. As word travels about what Hellen is doing, demand for her services is growing. She has constructed a new brick building large enough for 10 women and their children, and she's clearly working to change the system, too: Hellen insists that everyone report her case to the police, who will keep statistics and ensure that, if needed, the women and children receive medical care.

In Cambodia, Somaly Mam survived her own abuse before starting an organization to help others. Sold to a brothel by the family she lived with (she was an orphan in that war-torn land), she marks the day that she watched a pimp kill her best friend as the one on which she vowed to break free. Her organization—Agir pour les Femmes en Situation Précaire (AFESIP, "Acting for Women in Distressing Situations")—saves girls, many of them with HIV, from brothels in Cambodia, Thailand, Laos, and Vietnam. Somaly's life is under constant threat, but she knows she can really help these girls. She understands what they are going through, including the desire to return to the brothel; freedom is so completely unfamiliar that it is often, at least initially, unwelcome. "All I want to do is help these girls—to be a true mother to them, someone who gives them love."

Abused, orphaned, and destitute children in Jaipur, India, now have somewhere to go, thanks to Adha Goswami. The place is named Ladli, and to call it a sanctuary doesn't go far enough. There, boys and girls who have been struggling to survive each day are fed, clothed, housed, given medical treatment, and compassionate care—some for the first time in their lives. When they are ready, they also get basic education and vocational training: Jaipur has a long tradition of jewelry making, and the youth also learn tailoring and needlework. Most importantly, the children develop social skills and build confidence and self-esteem. After Adha's professional career, creation of this oasis in a poor desert city was an important project for her; her own mother died before she was two, and she was orphaned at 18.

Living rough, of course, is not just a problem in developing countries—residents of any Western city have seen homeless people, too. In the United States alone, approximately 750,000 people are homeless on any given night. It's a huge problem and, with the mortgage crisis in the United States, some observers believe it's going to get worse. But don't tell New Radical Innovator John Hickenlooper that. He's mayor of Denver, Colorado, one of the country's most beautiful cities. When he took office, residents and tourists were handing over more than $4 million each year to panhandlers, and the city was spending $70 million to help the homeless. The mayor launched an ambitious new plan to house the down-and-out rather than giving them handouts. The program—funded by both private and public sources—is working, and it is saving the city about $1.5 million a year. Cleverly recognizing that people still wanted to contribute, John decided to install parking meters to collect their donations. When you deposit money into the specially marked meters, the needle moves from "despair" to "hope" and every penny goes to the homeless fund. There are about 80 meters in place now, each bringing in about $2,000 a month.

Leadership

Leaders come in the most surprising shapes and sizes. When Craig Kielburger was just 12, he learned about the murder of a Pakistani child laborer. Deeply disturbed by this news, he immediately started an organization to help free children from poverty, exploitation, and powerlessness. Free the Children began as a group of classmates and has grown into an international organization. Craig and his brother Marc run the organization, which is helping more than 1 million youth in 45 countries. Unlike any other children's charity, Free the Children is both funded and managed by young people. One of its many programs involves working with students at schools across North America, encouraging them to act both locally and globally as agents of change. These young people are becoming the Next New Radicals before our eyes.

And then there are those who continue to make a contribution well beyond traditional retirement age. I'm thinking of Walter Cronkite, a respected and beloved news anchor who was a comforting presence in North American homes for decades, who has just announced, at 90 years of age, that he's negotiating to return to television. He'll be at our party, and I'll bet he brings the man whose New Radical idea he wholeheartedly supports. I'm talking about Ohio Congressman Dennis Kucinich, who proposed the creation of a U.S. Department of Peace. A Cabinet-level department, it would advise the Secretary of Defense and the Secretary of State on all matters relating to national security, including the protection of human rights and the prevention of, amelioration of, and deescalation of unarmed and armed international conflict. The department would operate domestically, too—addressing violence in our streets, homes, and schools, as well as proposing solutions for the so-called war on drugs. "To some," says the newsman, "this will sound terribly naive, given the current state of things and the very real changes that face us. But the real naiveté may just be with those who believe military force will make us safe." To whit, there are now 65 congressional cosponsors for the U.S. Department of Peace legislation. Walter and the other Americans who have formed the Peace Alliance to support the creation of this new federal department point out that there is ample science that shows that there are practical and effective ways for people to resolve their differences without violence. They point to the significant growth in peace and conflict resolution studies at universities around the world as evidence of a growing support for this idea.

No party is complete without a surprise guest or two. I started this coda with a 93-year-old New Radical, and I will end it with a group of leaders who have 1,000 years of collective experience to offer. I'm referring, of course, to the small group of luminaries who have come together to create the breathtaking Council of Elders.

Their number include former South African president Nelson Mandela, former U.N. secretary-general Kofi Annan, Archbishop Desmond Tutu, former Irish president Mary Robinson, former U.S. president Jimmy Carter, Indian women's rights campaigner Ela Bhatt, former Norwegian prime minister Gro Harlem Brundtland, former Chinese envoy to the United Nations Li Zhaoxing, Bangladeshi microcredit pioneer Muhammad Yunus, and longtime campaigner for children's rights Graca Machel. In announcing their undertaking, they also said that a chair had been left empty for Burmese opposition leader Aung San Suu Kyi, who has been under house arrest for more than a decade (and who is making headlines again as Buddhist monks and citizens take to the streets to protest a repressive regime).

In such uncertain times, these elders are our living link to tradition and a powerful reminder of deeply held and universal human principles and values. As I wrapped up the writing of this book, they were meeting to discuss their priorities.

I must tell you, in closing, that when I first heard about the formation of this council, Hokusai's Great Wave immediately came to mind. To me, that print and this gesture both convey the same message. Look, they are saying, let's not fool ourselves: we are in trouble, and we face a huge and frightening wave. But, at the same time, it is not beyond us. We are seasoned "fishermen," and if we work together, we will survive. For we are the New Radicals.

Bonus Chapter 2

New Radical Worksheets

Indo-Pacific coral reefs are disappearing twice as fast as the world's rainforests. In the 1980s, approximately 40 percent of reefs in these oceans were covered with live coral. Today, just 2 percent are. And an exposed reef—that is, one not covered with live tissue—erodes more quickly.

—*New Scientist*, August 2007

CHAPTER 1: ARE YOU A NEW RADICAL?

Check-in

Are you a New Radical-in-the-making? Check and see how many of these apply.

General

___ I want my work to be meaningful.
___ I want it to reflect my values.
___ I want to make a difference in the world.
___ I want work that I feel passionate about.
___ I'm concerned about the state of the world and believe that it's possible to make a difference, one act at a time.
___ I'm hopeful about the future and believe that constructive solutions to our problems are possible.
___ I want to connect with other like-minded people.
___ I want to try new things and to stretch myself.

Midlife or older

___ I intend to keep working and to stay active and engaged.
___ I believe that I have much to contribute.
___ I'm feeling at the top of my game.
___ I want to leave a legacy.
___ I believe my greatest contribution is yet to come.

New Radicals cover a wide spectrum, from mildly to wildly radical. Where do you see yourself on this continuum? And what is of interest to you now?

___ I see myself as being mildly radical (a simple transition, within easy reach).

___ I want to be wildly radical (a profound, life-altering transformation).

___ I'm somewhere in between.

___ I want to become an Activist (such as working for a nonprofit organization).

___ I want to be an Entrepreneur (starting a new venture).

___ I want to be an Innovator (working for change from inside).

Reflections

- How did I respond when I discovered this book?
- Does the first chapter describe me, or who I'd like to be?
- Have I seen examples of the New Radicals movement?

Notes:

CHAPTER 2: HOW DO YOU GET STARTED?

Few people roll out of bed one morning wanting to save the world. Instead, wake-up calls rouse us and set us on a path toward becoming a New Radical.

Category One: Stirred

We feel a gentle nudge, or an invitation to rouse ourselves from what's familiar.

PROFILE OF KEVIN SALWEN, *MOTTO* MAGAZINE

WAKE-UP	Had risen to top of organization. Began to notice subtle changes in his behavior. Realized that he was not making the most of his capacity and capabilities.
RESEARCH	Was staying at *Wall Street Journal (WSJ)* an option?
DECISION	Start a company with another *WSJ* alumnus.
RESEARCH	Continued to talk about changing media landscape. Spotted gaping hole: business media "from neck up"
DECISION	Started *Motto* magazine, "purpose, passion, profit"
BOTTOM LINE	Dual mission: to make the world a better place and to make money for its investors.

Category Two: Shaken

A powerful inner voice or external event disrupts our lives.

PROFILE OF ROCCO ROSSI, HEART AND STROKE FOUNDATION

WAKE-UP	Beloved mentor died of heart attack at the age of 44.
INSIGHT	A voyage of discovery, including a trip around New Zealand and two walks along Camino Frances.
RESEARCH	Volunteered for friend's political campaign. Talked to colleagues, contacts, and search firms.
DECISION	Work in the service sector.
RESEARCH	Looking for nonprofit group large enough to be challenging and meet his financial needs. Looking for personal connection.
DECISION	Lead the Heart and Stroke Foundation.
BOTTOM LINE	Service with a personal connection.

Category Three: Devastation

Life delivers a blow that wreaks havoc.

PROFILE OF ELIZABETH AND STEPHEN ALDERMAN, PETER C. ALDERMAN FOUNDATION

WAKE-UP	Peter, their son, died in the attacks at the World Trade Center on September 11, 2001.
REFLECTION	Wanted to honor his memory.
RESEARCH	Considered and rejected several options. Saw item on *Nightline* that inspired them.
DECISION	Started a foundation to help survivors of trauma.
BOTTOM LINE	Profound good as a way to counter profound evil.

The following check-in and reflections will help you to think about your own wake-up call, assess how you feel about this journey, and determine what you can do to prepare for it.

Check-in

___ My work no longer holds the same appeal.

___ I want to leave a legacy.

___ Something major has happened in my life.

___ I'm determined to see what's happened (no matter how painful or disruptive) in positive terms. I believe good will come of it.

___ I have/want to have a positive view of the world.

___ I will respond to this wake-up call by reinventing my work.

___ I don't have any idea what my new role might be, but I'm looking forward to discovering it.

___ I need time to think about what I might do.

___ I know what my new role might be and need help to make it happen.

___ I recognize that I've been changed by this experience.

___ I'm making a commitment to this journey.

___ I'm preparing for the journey.

___ I'm dropping, delegating, or postponing things to create time and space.

___ I will establish a support system for myself.

___ I will help others on their journey.

___ I will be alert to synchronicity.

Reflections

- How and when did my wake-up call come?
- How do I feel about the work I am doing now? What's changed?
- What do I want to do with the rest of my life?

- Do I want to leave a legacy? What would that look like?
- Do I know anyone else who is having similar thoughts and experiences?
- Am I ready to create something new in my life?
- Do I want to become a New Radical? Or, for now, do I simply want to read about others who have done so?
- Am I open to inspiration? To synchronicity?
- Is my self-concept changing? Am I discovering hidden capabilities? If so, what are they?
- Have I changed? Are my heart and mind more open to others? What's a good example?
- Are my priorities and philosophies changing? How? What's different?
- What are my thoughts and feelings about the journey ahead? What am I looking forward to? What do I fear most?
- How can I find people to support me? How might we support one another?
- How can I manage people who might try to hold me back? What might their reasons be?

Notes:

CHAPTER 3: WHAT DO YOU HAVE TO OFFER?

New Radicals begin their journey with an inventory of what they bring to the table.

Skills

What are your abilities? And how might they become a portfolio of transferable skills?

PROFILE OF JAMIE KENNEDY, JAMIE KENNEDY KITCHENS

WAKE-UP	Restaurant industry seemed unsustainable.
INSIGHT	A market for local growers and producers would help.
DECISION	Change menu daily, based on what's available.
INSIGHT	Shorter growing season could be addressed by taking historic approach.
DECISION	Five-mile (8-kilometer) radius for newest restaurant.
BOTTOM LINE	Establish a regional cuisine.

Strengths

What are your strengths? How can you use them in your new role?

PROFILE OF DR. MARK GRABOWSKY, CENTERS FOR DISEASE CONTROL AND GLOBAL FUND

WAKE-UP	While in Peace Corps, noticed students often too ill to come to class.

DECISION	Become a doctor.
INSIGHT	Measles is killing millions in Africa. All people need is a measles vaccine.
DECISION	Work with the World Health Organization to deliver continentwide campaign.
INSIGHT	Virtual organization is the way to tackle large-scale, complex issues.
DECISION	Tackle malaria with an integrated campaign.
BOTTOM LINE	The greatest good for the greatest number.

Working Together in New Ways

Are you comfortable moving between sectors? Are you open to fresh ideas and innovative solutions?

PROFILE OF SCOTT JOHNSON, MYELIN REPAIR FOUNDATION

WAKE-UP	Read an article about myelin repair research.
INSIGHT	Current research system doesn't work.
DECISION	Found Myelin Repair Foundation. Put together cross-disciplinary team of scientists. Create a new research model that delivers better results, faster.
BOTTOM LINE	The model works and can be applied to any disease.

The following check-in and reflections will help you to think about what you bring to the table.

Check-in

___ I know what I'm good at.

___ I understand that my skills are transferable.

___ I'm clear about which of these capabilities I want to use in my new role.

___ I see myself using my skills in a similar position in a new organization.

___ I believe that my first and second careers can work in tandem.

___ I know what my strengths are. (To assess, see Resources for tools.)

___ I know how to apply them.

___ I'm clear about which strengths I want to use as a New Radical.

___ I'm comfortable talking to my peers in different sectors.

___ I know what my New Radical role is, and I want to get started now.

___ I need more time to think more deeply about myself and what the world needs.

Reflections

- Looking back, what have I learned in my first career? What would I tell my twenty-something self that he or she didn't—couldn't—know? What has experience taught me?
- What career milestones come to mind?
- What are my most significant accomplishments? What were they the result of (for example, strategy, innovation, risk)? What made them so important? What made them satisfying to me?
- What was most important in others eyes? Why?
- What awards or other special recognition did I earn?
- What are my talents? What do I excel at? How would I describe my expertise?

- Do I understand which skills are transferable?
- How have I used my strengths at work? How would I like to use them in the future?
- What do I want to make use of in my New Radical role?
- Have I learned from my failures? Which have been my best teachers?
- Am I interested in what others would say I'm good at? How might I ask for their input?
- Have I observed new capabilities emerging recently? Do I believe they will?
- Is my capacity most important? Or is character what counts?
- Do I believe I have the power to make a difference?
- Do I have any idea now what my new role might be? Do I imagine it will be something similar, totally different, or a way to merge my old and new lives? Do I need more time to reflect and research?
- In Chapter 1, one of the check-ins asked if I felt I had "much to contribute." Is my answer the same now?

Notes:

CHAPTER 4: WHAT MOVES YOU?

As New Radicals, we want our work to reflect our values, and knowing more about our deeper selves improves our chances of success.

Childhood Dreams

What did you want to be when you grew up?

PROFILE OF DAN O'BRIEN, BROKEN HEART RANCH

DREAM	While on holiday with parents, he fell in love with America's Great Plains. He wanted to live there.
WAKE-UP	After years of farming, a series of financial and spiritual crises occurred—plus a divorce.
DECISION	Switch to buffalo ranching.
RESEARCH	Learn about native ecology. Find out how to keep, harvest, and market buffalo.
INSIGHT	Use wine model for marketing.
BOTTOM LINE	Restoring the Great Plains to their natural grandeur.

Living by Your Values

What are your values? Are they appropriate for your emerging New Radical self?

PROFILE OF KYE MARSHALL, MUSIC PSYCHOTHERAPIST

WAKE-UP	Playing in orchestra lost its allure. Longed for more meaningful work.
INSIGHT	Psychotherapy helped; could this be new role?
EXPLORATION	Studied psychotherapy. Developed improvisational skills. Began to compose jazz.
INSIGHT	All three interests could work together.
DECISION	Become a psychotherapist using music as a primary tool.
BOTTOM LINE	Music is a powerful healer.

Make Your Heart Sing

What is your bliss? When do you experience flow?

PROFILE OF JOHANN KOSS, RIGHT TO PLAY

WAKE-UP	Discovered children who didn't play.
DECISION	Found organization to help bring play—and joy—into the lives of disadvantaged children.
INSIGHT	More than games and sport. Also education, health care. And a sense of belonging.
EVOLUTION	Right to Play will help Western youth get into shape.
BOTTOM LINE	Play saves lives.

The following check-in and reflections will help you to find ways to connect with your deeper self and to consider how you might incorporate your values into your new role.

Check-in

___ I want to get to know my deeper self.

___ I'm making time and creating the conditions that will allow this to happen.

___ I'm taking time off and going somewhere I can explore who I truly am.

___ I'm keeping a journal.

___ I have started meditating.

___ I'm exploring the arts.

___ I'm talking about this part of the process with people who understand and will support me in it.

___ I always knew what I wanted to be when I grew up.

___ I no longer do certain things I did when I was younger, nor am I in touch with certain parts of myself; I long to return to these experiences.

___ I'm very aware of the values that were instilled in me.

___ I'm reflecting on them and deciding if I need a new belief system.

___ I know where my bliss lies.

___ I'm figuring out where my bliss lies.

___ I'm paying attention to when I feel flow in my life and work.

___ I look for ways to use the New Radicals credo (Positive, Constructive, Hopeful) in my life and work.

___ I'm working on my own personal New Radicals credo.

Reflections

- Who am I? What do I know about my deepest self? What gives my life meaning and purpose?
- Why might the answers not readily come to mind? Or do I know, but have been keeping the answers to myself?
- How can I create the conditions that will allow me to explore this inner terrain? What can I do at home? Might I go away?
- What does *inner work* mean to me? What works best for me?
- Are there others who can support me?
- When I was little, what did I want to be when I grew up?
- Did I have an experience or role model that shaped me? Who are the people who inspired me when I was young? Who inspires me now?
- What are my favorite movies and books? Do they contain clues about the life I'd like to lead?
- Do I have an unexplored, pent-up dream? What would I like to try?
- What have I forgotten about myself?
- What stories do I live by?
- What home truths come back to me time and again?
- Are these beliefs relevant to me today? Are they relevant to what I want to become?
- How might I incorporate them in my new role?
- Do I experience bliss at work? When and under what circumstances do I do so? How might I incorporate this in my new role?
- What about flow? Do I recognize it? Have I felt it? How might I repeat the experience?
- Have these experiences influenced my work? my relationships at work?

- Have I met others who know about bliss and flow? Might we talk about our experiences?
- How can I incorporate bliss into my new role?
- What about flow?
- How do I feel about the New Radicals credo? Does it make sense to me?
- Have I found ways to apply it in my life?
- Am I interested in developing a code of my own?
- Is there a need for a third kind of intelligence in our world? What might that look like?
- Do I share Dr. Coles's optimism about the world?
- Do I now have a better sense of what moves me? Do I know what values I want to incorporate in my new role?

Notes:

____

____

____

____

____

____

____

____

CHAPTER 5: WHAT DOES THE WORLD NEED?

The world needs so much that the effort to improve it can seem overwhelming. How do you decide what to do?

Start with a Deep Passion

What does your heart tell you?

PROFILE OF WENDY KOPP, TEACH FOR AMERICA

INSIGHT	Not everyone has same educational opportunities. This could change, with help of best and brightest students.
RESEARCH	Talked to students, school boards, sponsors.
DECISION	Found national agency to recruit and place students in rural and inner-city schools.
EVOLUTION	New Teachers Project.
BOTTOM LINE	Education can change a life.

Start Close to Home

What needs tending to in our own backyards?

PROFILE OF DON STANNARD-FRIEL, NOTRE DAME DE NAMUR UNIVERSITY

WAKE-UP	Needed a break from teaching. Spent time in Tenderloin district of San Francisco. Got to know community.
INSIGHT	Everything he'd learned throughout his life could come together in one role.

DECISION	Teach students about inner-city issues and people in such a neighborhood.
EVOLUTION	Series of programs for residents, in cooperation with community and police.
BOTTOM LINE	It's all about making a difference in one person's life.

Start with What Cries Out for Help

What compels you, making your course of action obvious?

PROFILE OF DR. VICTORIA HALE, INSTITUTE FOR ONEWORLD HEALTH

INSIGHT	Most of world doesn't have the pharmaceutical industry working for it.
WAKE-UP	Sense of mastery, achieved goals. Lost enthusiasm for current work. Longing to do something more stimulating and meaningful. Yearning to make a difference.
RESEARCH	Talked to biotech company founders. Talked to people in world health. Looked for promising drug candidates.
INSIGHT	For-profit model would present the same problems as before.
DECISION	Found the world's first nonprofit pharmaceutical company, OneWorld Health.
EVOLUTION	Several multinational pharmaceutical companies want to partner with OneWorld Health.
BOTTOM LINE	Can save the world, one disease at a time.

The following check-in and reflections will help you to shape your understanding of the issues and begin to discover where you might help.

Check-in

___ I sometimes feel overwhelmed by the enormity of the problems. What can one person do?

___ I don't know where to begin. How might I help?

___ I'm giving myself time to find the answer.

___ I believe every small gesture makes a difference.

___ I'm reading media sources that are new to me, as a way to broaden my awareness.

___ I'm meeting new people to find out more about what's going on.

___ I'm paying attention to what I'm passionate about.

___ I'm looking at what's going on in my community.

___ I notice what cries out for help.

Reflections

- What captivates me? What's absolutely fascinating?
- What do I feel passionate about?
- What alarms or distresses me?
- What issues make me want to come up with innovative solutions?
- What's going on in the world that I'd like to know more about? How might I learn more?
- What need do I see in my community? Who needs help? Who is trying so hard but needs a little extra help?
- What good ideas are out there that I might expand on?
- What can I read that I normally don't make time for?

- Who might I meet and talk to who can help me in my search for information and answers?
- Can I keep my horizon wide open for now? Do I trust that it will narrow naturally over time?
- Do I think the world is in crisis? Is the case for action getting louder?
- Am I ready to make a decision about my new role?
- Do I need to revisit any of the earlier stages first? Do I have a good grasp of my abilities? Do I have insight into what's important to me now? Do I know how I want to help—what I'm ready to devote myself to, whether in my community, my country, or around the world?

Notes:

CHAPTER 6: WHAT IS YOUR NEW ROLE?

New Radicals are eager to choose a new role that combines their deepest desires with their hard-won capabilities. How to decide?

Take the Natural Next Step

Is there an obvious choice?

PROFILE OF DON RAYMOND, CANADA PENSION PLAN INVESTMENT BOARD (CPPIB)

WAKE-UP	Looking for an intellectual challenge. Also seeking a way to give back.
DECISION	Become senior vice president and head of public market investments of the CPPIB.
INSIGHT	The Policy on Responsible Investing was a smart financial move.
RESEARCH	Worked with the United Nations on development of its Principles of Responsible Investing.
EVOLUTION	CPPIB is also a signatory to the Carbon Disclosure Project.
BOTTOM LINE	These are financial decisions.

Watch for a Flash of Inspiration

Have you had a bolt out of the blue?

PROFILE OF SUZANNE SEGGERMAN, GAMES FOR CHANGE

WAKE-UP	Time is precious. Wants to do only meaningful things.

INSIGHT	Digital games are a powerful way to engage people with serious content. The size of the games sector is significant.
DECISION	Cofound Games for Change.
BOTTOM LINE	Creating an environment where meaningful games will thrive.

Achieve a Breakthrough

Might everything you've done come together in a new role?

PROFILE OF DR. ED SUTT, STANLEY-BOSTITCH

INSIGHT	Fasteners fail.
RESEARCH	Earned degrees. Got hands-on experience.
DECISION	Reinvent the nail.
INVENTION	HurriQuake nail.
BOTTOM LINE	The nails stay in place even under duress of a hurricane or an earthquake.

The following check-in and reflections will help you to decide what your role might be.

Check-in

___ I'm looking over my shoulder at my first career.
___ I'm ready to choose or create my New Radical role.
___ I have been offered a New Radical role.
___ I know what my New Radical role will be.
___ I need more time to explore before I decide.
___ I want to be an Activist (actively serving the less fortunate).

___ I want to be an Entrepreneur (start a new enterprise designed to make a difference).

___ I want to become an Innovator (drive change from inside).

___ I'm making a list of options and weighing the pros and cons of each.

___ I see my new role as a natural next step.

___ I have had a flash of inspiration.

___ Everything comes together in this new role.

___ I can see that my role will continue to evolve.

Reflections

- How do I feel now that I'm about to become a New Radical?
- Do I feel I have something to contribute? (How has my answer changed since I responded to the same question for Chapter 1?)
- When I look back at my first career, what comes to mind? What feelings arise? What do I most appreciate about it? What am I happy to leave behind?
- Am I ready to move on and create or choose a new role for myself?
- Whose work fascinates me? Whose accomplishment do I admire?
- What would a rewarding role look like? (How has my answer changed since I began reading this book?)
- How would I like to spend each day?
- What would make me leap out of bed and race toward my destination at high speed? What need would I happily meet? What would make me feel connected to something more important?
- What clues do I have that I can follow as I decide? Have I had any flashes of inspiration?
- Can I see the intersections between what I have to offer and what the world needs?
- What skills and strengths might I use?

- How might I ensure that my new role is aligned with my values?
- Is my new role a natural next step?
- Am I ready to become an Activist? Do I know what's involved?
- Why an Entrepreneur? What appeals to me? Do I have what it takes?
- Have I carefully considered whether being an Innovator is for me? Can I redesign my current role so that it has more meaning? Whom would I have to talk to about this? How could I make the case? How might I work with others toward this goal?
- Can I talk to my support team about my ideas? Will they help me decide?
- How might my new role change over time? Do I want to keep growing and evolving in the years to come? How will the organization I'm going to be affiliated with change? How might I? What do I want to be doing 10 years from now? How might I prepare for that today?
- Have I experienced or am I looking forward to the kind of "vital engagement" that Mihalyi Czikszentmihalyi writes about?
- What about the community of New Radicals? Am I beginning to find others who are on the path, too?
- Do I truly believe that my greatest contribution is yet to come? What might that be?

Notes:

CHAPTER 7: HOW DO YOU GET THERE FROM HERE?

You've chosen a role and need to figure out how to make it happen. Or you're trying to decide and need to maintain momentum.

Right Qualifications

What's the "union card" for your new role? Do you need experience? Education?

PROFILE OF MARK BRAYNE, DART CENTER

INSIGHT	First career as foreign correspondent: "not me."
WAKE-UP	Covering fall of Nicolae Ceausescu, dictator of Romania. Explosion of brotherly love on the streets of Bucharest. A personal emotional breakthrough, and long-hidden unhappiness revealed.
RESEARCH	Began to study psychotherapy. Found that psychotherapy is a way to understand self, and considered it as a second career.
INSIGHT	Don't abandon first career, but combine the two: news reporting and psychotherapy.
DECISION	Become a psychotherapist working with journalists and news organizations.
BOTTOM LINE	Journalists who understand trauma are safer—and better at their work.

Right People

Do you have the right people on your team? in your network? in your new organization?

PROFILE OF DAVID SIMMS, BRIDGESTAR

WAKE-UP	Mission-driven self: "This isn't what you're called to do."
RESEARCH	Put out feelers, including database of former employer.
INSIGHT	Perfect combination of skills: corporate and social. Huge demand: meeting talent needs of non-profit groups.
DECISION	Become managing partner of Bridgestar, a placement firm.
BOTTOM LINE	Instead of creating wealth, making a world of difference.

The following check-in and reflections will help you to plan the final steps you need to take.

Check-in

___ I'm mapping out the steps I need to take to become a New Radical.

___ I recognize the value of planning.

___ I'm creating a plan that spells out my goals, breaks these into actionable steps, and incorporates a timeline.

___ I'm doing my homework to determine if the role I have in mind (and the new environment) is the right fit.

___ I'm assessing whether I have the right qualifications.

___ I'm aware of the importance of the right attitude when entering new territory, whether as a leader or otherwise—that humility is key and will help me in my new role.

___ I have established a good network, or I am working on this.

___ I'm getting to know people in the area I want to work, or even in the precise organization.

___ I'm thinking about the kinds of skills my team will need, and looking around for people to fill the bill.

___ I'm sorting out my finances so that I can fund the transition.

Reflections

- What steps do I need to take to become a New Radical?
- What will my plan include? What are my goals? What can I do to achieve them? What's a realistic timeline?
- Do I need more experience before attempting this new role? Where and how might I get this experience?
- Do I need to go back to school to get more qualifications? Am I excited about this? Do I love learning?
- How much do I know about my new role? About the environment? About what would be required of me?
- How might people in my new working environment respond to me? Do we have similar worldviews or ways of approaching challenges?
- Is it difficult for me to lose my sense of mastery or to learn new ways of working? Or do I relish it?
- How might I avoid the Stockholm syndrome—the behavior over time where the captive becomes sympathetic to the captor?
- Do I have financial resources on which I can draw? Savings? Retirement funds? Perhaps an early inheritance?
- Can I juggle my existing career while I work toward my new one?
- Will the role I have in mind pay me enough? If not, how might I either change my lifestyle or supplement my income?
- Is there another way to look at money? Is it the most important metric?

- Does struggling toward a cherished goal help me to develop further and discover new parts of myself? Is Jonathan Haidt right when he talks about the value of diversity? Has my view of this topic changed since Chapter 2?
- Am I aware of new capabilities emerging? If so, what are they? Do I need to incorporate them in my new role?
- How might I stay connected to everything I've learned about myself and what I want to do with the rest of my life?
- Am I building in regular time for reflection? Will I reassess my plan from time to time?

Notes:

CHAPTER 8: HOW DO YOU MAKE A NAME FOR YOURSELF?

Making the case for why you're the ideal person for the New Radical role.

Who Are You?

What is your core identity or character? What do you stand for?

PROFILE OF MELISSA DYRDAHL, BRING LIGHT

WAKE-UP	Career was no longer challenging.
INSIGHT	Working with charities is a blissful experience.
DECISION	Start a company with a new take on charitable giving.
RESEARCH	Talked to nonprofits.
BOTTOM LINE	Spread hope and bring light into people's lives.

PROFILE OF DREW MCMANUS, BRING LIGHT

DECISION	Start a company.
RESEARCH	Looked into philanthropic trends. Psychology/sociology of giving.
INSIGHT	New model could be more interactive. Opportunity for social networking should be included.
BOTTOM LINE	Make it easier—and more interesting—for people to give.

What Do You Do?

What is your extended identity, or capacity? What do you do well?

PROFILE OF PAUL GILLESPIE, KIDS' INTERNET SAFETY ALLIANCE (KINSA)

INSIGHT	Internet changed child porn trade and policing.
DECISION	Ask Microsoft for help. Create database, Child Exploitation Tracking System (CETS).
EVOLUTION	Create a nonprofit, the Kids' Internet Safety Alliance (KINSA). Work as a consultant to bring ideas around the world.
BOTTOM LINE	Big name needs to help bring issue out of closet. Do what Elizabeth Taylor did for AIDS.

What Can You Do for Me?

What is your potential identity? How might you help?

PROFILE OF PATTY JOHNSON, NORTH SOUTH PROJECT

INSIGHT	Indigenous skills were not fully appreciated. Thought there might be another way: fusion of northern sensibilities and southern skills.
RESEARCH	Got to know companies in developing countries.
DECISION	Found North South Project, based on true partnerships with people in developing countries.
BOTTOM LINE	Design can make a difference in people's lives.

The following check-in and reflections will help you to articulate your New Radical brand.

Check-in

___ I have a good sense of my core identity or character: my strengths, values, and what I stand for.

___ I can answer the question, "Who are you?"

___ I have a good grasp of what I bring to the table: my knowledge and expertise.

___ I can answer the question, "What do you do?"

___ I believe that my midlife self has advantages over my younger self.

___ I have a clear idea of how I can make a difference in this world.

___ I can answer the question, "What can you do for me?"

___ I want to be inspired, to feel hopeful, to lead a meaningful life.

___ I feel we are poised on the verge of a positive, constructive, hopeful new age.

___ I believe I can find more meaning and help save the world.

Reflections

- Have I learned enough about my character—thinking back to Chapter 4—to be able to articulate it?
- How do I feel putting this into words and knowing that it will be important to others?
- Have I heard about my core identity from others? Do I need to incorporate their thoughts?
- What was it like to reflect on my experiences and what I have learned? Am I ready to articulate my capacity to others?
- What might the advantages of midlife be? Do we now have the expertise, knowledge, and resources about which we once only dreamed? Do others share my view? Have I had an experience of this already?

- Can I see clearly the ways that my character and capacity can come together in a role that might make a world of difference?
- Can I put this insight into words?

Notes:

CHAPTER 9: ARE YOU READY?

Thousands, perhaps tens of thousands, of New Radicals are criss-crossing the planet, doing good works. It's time to decide if you're ready to take the final step.

Check-in

___ I see now that I'm not alone, that there are others like me who are reinventing their work and saving the world.
___ I see the connections between people doing good works all over the world.
___ I'm ready. Yes, I want to become a New Radical!
___ I need to wait a bit and take care of some important details in my life.
___ I understand that becoming a New Radical will change my life and make an enormous difference in the lives of others.
___ I see that the baby boomers have made a contribution: a quiet revolution in social values.
___ I know that the answer to the question "when will the tipping point come?" rests with me and other New Radicals-in-the-making.
___ I will do everything I can to live by and spread the New Radicals credo: positive, constructive, hopeful.

Reflections

- Am I ready to become a New Radical? (Has my answer changed while I was reading this book?)
- Are there things I need to attend to first?
- Might I be looking for ways to avoid taking this final step, or are my reasons for delay valid?
- I have read what New Radical pioneers have to say. What might my "Top 10 Reasons to Become a New Radical" be?

- What has the baby boom generation accomplished? What do I most admire about my parent's generation? My children's?
- When do I think the tipping point will come?
- Am I ready to join the most powerful and influential movement of our times?

Notes:

Bliss meaning
Flow engagement
Vital engagement
have real impact

P 84 VINOD Khosla
mind-numbing
power-point presentation
P 175 Positive Sum Games
P 167 Snazzy Slide Show

Resources

BOOKS

Csikszentmihalyi, Mihaly, *Flow: The Psychology of Optimal Experience*, HarperPerennial, New York, 1990.

Ferrucci, Piero, *The Power of Kindness: The Unexpected Benefits of Leading a Compassionate Life*, Tarcher/Penguin, New York, 2006.

Fox, Matthew, *The Reinvention of Work: A New Vision of Livelihood for Our Time*, HarperCollins, New York, 1994.

Haidt, Jonathan, *The Happiness Hypothesis: Why the Meaningful Life Is Closer Than You Think*, Basic Books, New York, 2006.

Homer-Dixon, Thomas, *The Upside of Down: Catastrophe, Creativity, and the Renewal of Civilization*, Knopf Canada, Toronto, 2006.

Kabat-Zinn, Jon, *Full Catastrophe Living: Using the Wisdom of Your Body and Mind to Face Stress, Pain, and Illness*, Dell Publishing, New York, 1990.

———, *Wherever You Go There You Are: Mindfulness Meditation in Everyday Life*, Hyperion, New York, 1994.

———, *Coming to Our Senses: Healing Ourselves and the World through Mindfulness*, Hyperion, New York, 2005.

Seligman, Martin, *Learned Optimism: How to Change Your Mind and Your Life*, Free Press, Simon & Schuster, New York, 1990.

———, *Authentic Happiness: Using the New Positive Psychology to Realize Your Potential for Lasting Fulfillment*, Free Press, Simon & Schuster, New York, 2002.

Steinhorn, Leonard, *The Greater Generation: In Defense of the Baby Boom Legacy*, St. Martin's Press, New York, 2006.

Also recommended:

Buckingham, Marcus, and Donald O. Clifton, *Now, Discover Your Strengths*, Free Press, Simon & Schuster, New York, 2001.

Cameron, Julia, *The Artist's Way: A Spiritual Path to Higher Creativity*, Tarcher, New York, 1992.

Edwards, Betty, *Drawing on the Right Side of the Brain*, Tarcher, Los Angeles, 1979.

Losada, Isabel, *A Beginner's Guide to Changing the World: A True Life Adventure Story*, HarperCollins, New York, 2005.

Rath, Tom, *StrengthsFinder 2.0*, Gallup Press, New York, 2007.

Steffen, Alex, ed., *Worldchanging: A User's Guide for the 21st Century*, Harry N. Abrahms, New York, 2006.

MAGAZINES

Aware

GOOD

ODE

Resurgence

DVDs

Joseph Campbell and the Power of Myth, with Bill Moyers, Mystic Fire Video, 2001.

WEB SITES

The VIA Signature Strength Survey is a 246-question survey that measures 24 character strengths and helps you identify your 5 greatest qualities.

VIA Signature Strengths Questionnaire:
www.authentichappiness.sas.upenn.edu/

There are a number of Web sites that act as hubs and are ideal jumping-off points for further exploration.

Civic Ventures: www.civicventures.org

The Skoll Foundation: www.skollfoundation.org

Social Edge, a program of The Skoll Foundation:
www.socialedge.org

On the social networking side, try:

Zaadz: www.zaadz.com

For an overview of good works around the world, try this Wiki-like site:

Wiser Earth: www.wiserearth.org

For information and advocacy for people 50+:

In the United States, AARP: www.aarp.org

In Canada, CARP: www.carp.ca

SURVEYS

Merrill Lynch "The New Retirement Survey," February 22, 2005.

MetLife Foundation/Civic Ventures "New Face of Work Survey," June 16, 2005.

CHAPTER EPIGRAPH SOURCES

Chapter 1: "Search for Green Cremation in India," *The Economist,* International, June 24, 2007.

Chapter 2: Dugger, Celia W., "U.N. Predicts Urban Population Explosion," *New York Times,* June 28, 2007.

Chapter 3: Chong, Jia-Rui, and Thomas H. Maugh II, "Suddenly, the Bees Are Simply Vanishing," *Los Angeles Times,* June 10, 2007.

Scoffield, Heather, "Why Bees Are Important to Your Wallet," *Globe and Mail,* Investor Weekend, June 9, 2007.

Chapter 4: "Tidal Wave," *The Economist*, Europe, Valletta, Malta, June 2007.

Chapter 5: Watts, Jonathan, "Chinese Police Free 450 Slave Workers," *The Guardian Weekly,* International News, June 22, 2007.

Chapter 6: McCrummen, Stephanie, "'Safari' Threat to Ancient Tribe," *The Guardian Weekly,* International Development, June 22, 2007. Reprinted from the *Washington Post.*

Chapter 7: Williams, Frances, "Future Blighted by Environmental Damage, says UN," *Financial Times,* World News, June 23/24, 2007.

Chapter 8: Jowit, Juliette, and Javier Espinoza, "Natural Wonder under Threat," *The Guardian Weekly,* International News, June 22, 2007. Reprinted from the *Observer.*

Chapter 9: Ibbitson, John, "A Country Hung Out to Dry," *The Globe and Mail,* June 23, 2007.

Bonus Chapter 1: Wagner, Thomas, "Relief Agencies Say Nearly One-Third of Iraqis Need Emergency Care," Associated Press, July 30, 2007.

Bonus Chapter 2: Brahic, Catherine, "Coral Reefs Are Vanishing Faster than Rain Forests," *New Scientist,* Environment, August 8, 2007.

Index

C

D

E

F

G

N

O

ABOUT THE AUTHOR

Julia Moulden coined the phrase "New Radicals" and now helps individuals and organizations find new ways to do good works.

Her first book, *Green Is Gold* (HarperBusiness), was a bestseller about another emerging trend. The first environmental management guide for business, it was published in six countries. Her byline has also appeared in a diverse range of publications, including *Ms* magazine, the *Globe and Mail*, and *Toronto Life*.

Since 1985, she has written speeches for cabinet ministers, CEOs, and celebrities. Her clients include North America's leading organizations, including AstraZeneca, Four Seasons Hotels and Resorts, and Ford Motor Company.

Born in Toronto in 1956, Julia has lived in Europe, the United States, and Mexico. She kayaks as often as possible on Georgian Bay.

JOIN THE CONVERSATION

The New Radicals movement is just beginning. Please visit our Web site to share your story, learn about other New Radicals, and sign up for regular news and information updates. We'll even send you a free "I'm a New Radical" button! Details are online at www.WeAreTheNewRadicals.com.